JOLTS

JOLTS

THE TV WASTELAND AND THE CANADIAN OASIS

MORRIS WOLFE

James Lorimer & Company, Publishers
Toronto 1985

Design: Dragon's Eye Press

Illustrations are reproduced by permission of: Toronto Star Syndicate (frontispiece cartoon); Global Television Network (photo 12); Canadian Broadcasting Corporation (all other photographs).

Canadian Cataloguing in Publication Data

Wolfe, Morris
  Jolts: the TV wasteland and the Canadian oasis

ISBN 0-88862-649-5 (bound) — ISBN 0-88862-648-7 (pbk.)

1. Television broadcasting - Social aspects - Canada. 2. Television programs - Canada. 3. Television programs - United States. I. Title

PN1992.3.C3W65 1985   791.45'0971   C85-099407-1

James Lorimer & Company, Publishers
Egerton Ryerson Memorial Building
35 Britain Street
Toronto, Ontario M5A 1R7

Printed in Canada

5 4 3 2 1   85 86 87 88 89

Contents

for Jen, Benj and Menya
who've taught me more
about television
(and everything else)
than they realize

Acknowledgements

I'm grateful to Robert Fulford, who first suggested that I write about television, and to *Saturday Night, Books in Canada, TVO Plus* and *TV Guide*, where some of these thoughts first appeared. A dozen or so Canadian Clubs from Halifax to Victoria invited me to try out some of this material. So did the Canadian Studies programme at the University of Edinburgh. Financial assistance from the Ontario Arts Council helped me buy time to work on the manuscript and to pay for research help from Michèle Doucet, Rick Lash and Elizabeth Harrison. The Ontario College of Art, where I teach part-time, continued to support my eating habit throughout. The CBC provided access to clipping files and programmes. Jennifer Wolfe typed the manuscript. My editor, Ted Mumford, was the soul of patience.

Introduction:
On Writing About
Television

I

I wrote a monthly television column for *Saturday Night* for seven years. Although it never stopped being hard work — I write slowly even at the best of times — it was fun. I learned an enormous amount, not least of all about myself. When the column stopped being fun, I quit. I'd said everything I wanted to say in that context and it was time to move on to other things. In any case, I'm not sure that critics and columnists have a useful lifespan of more than a half dozen years or so. By that time you've seen it all before. You've said it all before. And you probably said it better the first time.

Although television is now well into its fourth decade, it has yet to produce a major critic. There is no one I know of now writing about television (at least in English) with the knowledge and love George Bernard Shaw showed toward music and Kenneth Tynan toward theatre or that Pauline Kael now shows toward film. By the time the movies were as old as television is now, there were already a number of major film critics on the scene, men and women who believed that film deserved the same serious treatment that books and plays were given. Happily, they found editors and readers who agreed with them. Since then there hasn't been a time when we've been without at least a few first-rate film critics writing in English.

But serious criticism of anything — sports, politics, music, whatever — depends on the tacit understanding between critic and audience that the subject matters. Such an understanding still doesn't exist when it comes to television. Although on average we spend something like twenty-five hours a week in front of our TV sets, we continue to think of television as something we can't take seriously. That's partly, I suspect, because its offerings come to us without our having to do anything other than push a button. Good capitalists that we are, we value only what we have to go out into the marketplace and pay for. (Of course, we delude ourselves in thinking that TV is free. We pay for it every time we buy a product that advertises on television.) I'd hoped our attitude would change with the advent of Pay-TV, but there's no indication that that's the case.

Most of us use reviews of other things — books, movies, plays, restaurants — as consumer guides for choosing what we read, see or eat. Until recently, reviews of TV programmes couldn't be used that way because they appeared either after a programme had been aired or just before a programme that didn't fit into one's schedule. The videocassette machine is changing that. Unlike books and movies which have always been available long after they've been reviewed, making it possible to compare one's own reactions with those of the critics years after their views have been committed to print, television programmes have been ephemeral, with a lifespan of a half hour or an hour. If they continued to exist, it was in archives inaccessible to the general public.

Furthermore, books, movies and plays are finite; they have clear beginnings and endings. We speak of reading *a* book, seeing *a* movie, going to *a* play. But we watch not *a* television programme, but television; somehow we regard TV as never-ending. Thus the TV critic who pre-screens a programme in a network viewing-room in order to write about it before it's broadcast is cheating. He or she is taking the programme out of the busy context in which almost everyone else sees it — a context of people talking and moving about. As Clive James, former television critic of the *Observer*, puts it, "One of the chief functions of a television critic is to stay at home and watch the programmes on an ordinary domestic receiver, just as his readers do. If he goes to official previews, he will meet producers and directors, start understanding their problems, and find himself paying the inevitable price for free sandwiches."

II

Those who write about television can have problems accepting the role. Take me, for example. When Robert Fulford, the editor of *Saturday Night*, asked me in 1973 if I would like to write a monthly television column for the magazine, I felt hurt. I wondered if maybe he was telling me in his kindly way that he wasn't happy with my work as a book reviewer. I thought of myself as a serious person and that writing about television was beneath me. What would my friends think?

Writing about television, I discovered, was far more difficult than writing about books. A book reviewer often specializes — in first novels or reference works or whatever. A drama critic watches perhaps five or six plays a week. A television critic can't function that way. He or she has to be interested in, and knowledgeable about, a wide variety of subjects — from sports to drama, from soap opera to grand opera, and from the politics of broadcasting to the differences between tape and film. Kenneth Tynan, commenting on the impossibility of TV criticism, once said, "A television critic would have to know everything, and who knows everything?"

I was lucky in being able to work with an editor who believed that it was worth paying someone to *try* to write serious television criticism. Most TV critics aren't so lucky; other editors assume that anyone who owns a TV set can handle the job. That attitude is partly the result of condescension, partly of fear. The print media continue to be wary of TV, which, after all, competes with them for advertising revenue.

When radio arrived on the scene in the 1920s, the print media were terrified that the new medium would take their advertisers away. Newspapers and magazines paid as little attention to radio as possible, even refusing to list or review radio programmes. (The first radio columnist to write for the *Globe* was hired not by the *Globe* itself but by Simpson's, which bought space in the paper and paid Frank Chamberlain to fill it.) Lobbyists for public broadcasting shrewdly played on the print media's fears. In the early 1930s the Canadian Broadcasting League, for example, pointed out in a pamphlet entitled *Radio Broadcasting: A Threat to the Press* that advertising was increasing rapidly on radio and decreasing in print. Something had to be done. Newspaper and magazine editorials soon began to argue that radio was too important to be left in the hands of advertisers and public broadcasters. So important an educational tool needed to be a public service. Enter the CRBC (Canadian Radio Broadcasting Commission) in 1932, and later the CBC (1936).

III

If you write about television, it's a rare day on which you don't receive two or three envelopes filled with detailed programme listings and profiles of stars, all written in a style that can be easily paraphrased — or just plain lifted. Given the quantity and variety of such material, one can actually write a television column without watching television. And it happens. Editors (and readers) who wouldn't tolerate reporting by press release in any other area of a newspaper regularly accept it from television columnists.

If you're writing about a movie, a play, a hockey game, your readers expect a connected piece of prose on the subject. A little essay. If you're writing about television, it's acceptable to churn out copy that looks like a print analogue of the medium itself — a number of unconnected itty-bitty paragraphs, many of them garnered from press releases. The whole column looks and reads like a series of TV commercials, which does nothing to change our belief that television isn't worth taking seriously.

No one has spoken more pointedly of the inadequacies of those who write about TV than Ron Haggart of the CBC's *the fifth estate*. Haggart, himself a former newspaper columnist, laments, "If television is an arid wasteland, the people who write about it are its tumbleweed. Lacking in care or commitment, they skim the landscape of their beat, pulled this way by the puffs of publicity, pushed that way by the momentary passions of pack journalism. Their work habits are lazy, their insights banal, their principles dominated by a mendacious (and largely boring) vitriol."

Many TV critics spend far too much time letting us know they're slumming. And because most of us feel guilty about how much television we watch, we accept their condescension. Michael Arlen wrote the "On Air" column that appeared irregularly in *The New Yorker*. "What Pauline Kael does for the movies, Michael Arlen does for TV," declared one review of a collection of Arlen's columns. But the comparison was foolish. Pauline Kael loves movies with a passion; even when she writes about films she hates, her affection for the medium is never in doubt. Arlen, on the other hand, never let us forget that he really didn't like television all that much. At one point he asked, "What can a critic do in the face of...work which has almost no substance [and where] it is generally understood that the work's creators have no ambitions for it beyond the simplest commerce?"

But isn't that true of almost all of everything? And isn't one of the chief functions of the critic to *make* distinctions between and among books or television programmes or whatever is being criticized? If Arlen believed that there were no distinctions worth making, that TV was, in fact, a wasteland, maybe he shouldn't have been a television critic.

IV

I can't say I learned to care about television the way I do about books or movies. But I did learn (to my surprise) that a day didn't go by when I couldn't find at least one and usually more programmes worth watching and writing about. And I came to see that in addition to individual programmes (and series) there were also a number of interesting themes a TV critic could write about: how old people (women, children) are portrayed on television; how TV has changed sports; whether it's reasonable to expect as much as we do of TV newscasts, given that the text of *The National* fills less than half a page of the *Globe and Mail*.

I found I wanted to use my column to explore the differences between Canadian and American culture. Like many other English Canadians, I'd discovered in the late 1960s and early 1970s that being a Canadian mattered to me. It wasn't exactly that it hadn't mattered before. In important ways I'd been shaped by such distinctively Canadian institutions as the CBC and Hart House at the University of Toronto. But that shaping had gone on almost unconsciously. The assassinations of John Kennedy and Martin Luther King, French-Canadian nationalism, George Grant's *Lament for a Nation*, Walter Gordon's *A Choice for Canada*, the coming to power of Richard Nixon, the war in Vietnam changed that. I found myself thinking far more consciously of the differences between English-Canadian and American culture.

One of the things I realized is that we English Canadians have the shortest memories of any nation on earth. (The Irish, who are unable to forget anything, it seems, have the longest.) So it's not surprising that we are constantly engaged in trying to figure out who we are. Several such attempts at self-definition have been made in the past decade and a half.

In *Survival* (1972), Margaret Atwood suggests that Canadian stories are far more likely to be not about those who made it, as American stories are, but about those who made it back — who survived some awful experience. The survivor, says Atwood, has nothing to show for his or her efforts, just gratitude for still being alive. At the end of Brian Moore's *The Luck of Ginger Coffey*, for example, Ginger realizes he's a failure, that he's not going anywhere. But he's finally grateful for what he has. "Didn't most men try and fail, weren't most men losers? Didn't damn near everyone have to face up someday to the fact that their ship would never come in? He had tried: he had not won....What did it matter? He would die in humble circs: It did not matter. There would be no victory for Ginger

Coffey, no victory big or little, for...he had learned the truth. Life was the victory...going on was the victory...."
At the end of Donald Shebib's film *Goin' Down the Road*, Peter and Joey are young men following Horace Greeley's advice and going (still further) west. But we know things will never get much better for them. Indeed, they may get worse.

Herschel Hardin's fine and too little known book, *A Nation Unaware* (1974), argues that in many ways Canadian culture has from the beginning been a public enterprise culture rather than a private enterprise one. We realized early that we had a choice if we were to survive as a nation between, as Graham Spry once put it, "the State or the United States." The CPR was built during the wave of cultural nationalism that followed Confederation. Another transcontinental link, public broadcasting, was established at the end of the wave of nationalism that followed the First World War. Both are examples of the extent to which we as a people have opted over and over again for collective action. We've always been Red Tories.

Edgar Z. Friedenberg makes a similar point in *Deference to Authority* (1980). His book didn't get nearly the attention it deserved because Friedenberg is a transplanted American; we don't like the idea of having an American tell us about ourselves. In *Deference to Authority* Friedenberg argues that Canadians have always been much more respectful of, and inclined to defer to, authority than Americans. Sometimes that's a good thing, as it was in the 1960s when we chose to accept collective responsibility for medical care. Sometimes it's scary, as it was in October 1970 when eighty-eight per cent of us approved Pierre Trudeau's decision to invoke the War Measures Act, which suspended civil liberties and threw 450 innocent

Quebeckers in jail. None was ever charged with a crime; none ever received an apology.

Perhaps the best and briefest account of the differences between Canadian and American culture is in the introduction to June Callwood's *Portrait of Canada* (1981). Drawing on the work of Kenneth McNaught, John Porter, Northrop Frye and others, she argues that the central fact of North American history is that there were fifteen British colonies in North America before 1776. Thirteen opposed British authority and became the United States. Two remained obedient to Britain — Quebec and Nova Scotia — and they eventually became Canada. The character of both countries was shaped by the American Revolution and the migrations that followed. Loyalists (conservatives) moved north to Canada. (In 1812, eighty per cent of the population of Toronto was of U.S. extraction.) Dissenters (individualists) moved south to the U.S.

The United States, Callwood continues, put its faith in the individual and got dazzling achievements at the cost of some individuals choosing to become outlaws; Canada put its faith in paternalism and police power at the cost of flair and private enterprise. We all know the striking difference in crime rates between the two countries. The result, writes sociologist Kaspar Naegele, is that "there seems to be a greater acceptance of limitation, of hierarchical patterns" in Canada than in the U.S. "There seems to be less optimism, less faith in the future, less willingness to risk capital or reputation." Canadians would rather keep their money under their mattresses than invest it in Canadian business.

One side of the border, writes Callwood, "has a policeman for a hero, the red-coated Mountie. The other celebrates mavericks. One country believes father is always right; the other may put a bullet in father's head....During the Klondike gold rush of the Nineties, the American town of Skagway in the Alaskan panhandle was run by a ruthless American gangster and gunfights in the streets were common. Across the border in Canada, Yukon mining towns were so law-abiding that a miner safely could leave his poke of gold in an unlocked cabin."

Callwood points out some lovely ironies. The American emblem is the fierce, high-flying eagle; Canada's emblem is the beaver — a dull, plodding animal that occasionally bites off its own testicles and stands under falling trees. Canada's national anthem was written by a man who left Canada for the U.S. and used his royalties to try to persuade other Canadians to do the same thing.

These are some of the characteristics of English-Canadian culture, and some of the differences between it and American culture that other writers have suggested in recent years. The list could go on. One could talk, for example, not only of the influence of history, but also of that of geography on our character and our art. *The Mystic North*, a recent exhibit at the Art Gallery of Ontario, revealed some remarkable similarities between landscape painting in Canada and in northern Scandinavia.

What I want to outline in the pages that follow is yet another approach: an examination of the differences between English-Canadian and American culture as one can perceive them simply by looking at TV. Because there's no doubt that differences are there to be seen. Television in Canada is yet again under government review — this time by a task force appointed by the Mulroney Conservatives. Its report is due early in 1986. This task force, I suspect, like the many committees and commissions that have preceded it, will devote all its time to the politics of broadcasting and almost none to watching and discussing programmes. Indeed, the members of the task force are probably such busy people that they rarely have time to watch television at all. (John Meisel, former chairman of the CRTC, once told me he'd never seen *Sesame Street*.)

I would argue that the single most important statement any of these commissions and study groups have made in the past twenty years appeared in the Fowler Committee report of 1965: "The only thing that really matters in broadcasting," said Fowler, "is programme content; all the rest is housekeeping." That statement has frequently been repeated, but its argument has never been followed. My eyes blur as I read the bureaucratic mumbo-jumbo that makes up most reports on broadcasting. They seem to have almost nothing to do with me and my TV set.

What follows then is a kind of counter-report — a view of the state of Canadian television by someone who's spent a fair amount of time over the past decade watching it.

The First Law of
Commercial Television

I

I became aware of what I call The First Law of Commercial Television one night in the spring of 1976 while watching the first tryout of *90 Minutes Live*, a CBC experiment in late-night television. The host of the programme was Peter Gzowski, whose relaxed and understated interviewing technique I was familiar with from his superb radio programme *This Country in the Morning*. Gzowski had succeeded in persuading Thomas Berger, who was then heading an inquiry into the proposed Mackenzie Valley pipeline, to appear on *90 Minutes Live*. That Berger was appearing on the show at all was a remarkable achievement; but now that he was on air, he was proving to be something of a problem. In response to a question from Gzowski, Berger began talking quietly, and at length, about what the Mackenzie Valley pipeline inquiry meant, what the issues were, what his role was. He wasn't telling those of us who'd been reading the papers anything we didn't know already, but that was all right. It was unreasonable to expect any fresh revelations. All the interview could possibly do was give us an impression of Berger the man.

If this had been radio, Berger's answers would probably have been all right with Peter Gzowski too. But this was television and, according to the rules of commercial television, nothing was happening. There weren't enough jolts. Gzowski was getting uptight; he looked as if he were getting frantic signals from his producer to make something happen. So he awkwardly demanded that Berger tell us what conclusions he'd come to. But the adversary approach doesn't suit Gzowski, and Berger, surprised by the change in Gzowski's tone, and quite properly unwilling to discuss his conclusions while the hearings were still underway, retreated into a kind of defensive banality. Mercifully, the interview soon ended.*

I was disappointed with Gzowski. Certainly *90 Minutes Live* turned out to be a much better show than one would have thought possible based on this one episode. (I'll have more to say about *90 Minutes Live* later.) Yet what he was trying to do was perfectly understandable. Given the number of jolts our viewing of U.S. television has conditioned us to expect, it's easy for Canadians to fall into the trap of trying to imitate the American style. American programmers discovered some time ago that most of us have short attention spans and that those attention spans can be easily manipulated. They realized that if a long time goes by without a jolt of verbal or physical or emotional violence on the screen, or if the picture doesn't change quickly enough as a result of a jolt of rapid editing or camera movement, or movement by people or objects within the frame, or if the soundtrack doesn't have enough decibels, viewers will switch to a channel and a programme that gives them more of those things. That's how almost all the top American shows get their audiences. They obey

---

* It seemed appropriate that Gzowski's interview with Berger be sandwiched between a high-wire act and singer Patsy Gallant doing an English version of Gilles Vigneault's "Mon Pays." The chorus of the translated version kept repeating the words "I'm a star in New York; I'm a star in L.A."

the First Law of Commercial Television: *Thou shalt give them enough jolts per minute (jpm's) or thou shalt lose them.*

Let me illustrate what I mean by describing the jpm content of an episode of an American programme that first appeared the same fall (1976) that *90 Minutes Live* began its run — *Charlie's Angels.* This particular episode had three murders and seven attempted murders (including one in a bed that blew up and another resulting from an exploding tennis ball); one accidental death (in a plane crash); two serious injuries (one in a fall from the top of an oil storage tank); seven acts of miscellaneous violence (including the release of poison gas); and five crimes — illegal entries, etc. — committed by the Angels themselves in the cause of justice. This list doesn't include other kinds of jolts — such as car chases and rapid editing — to say nothing of the sexual jolts for men provided by the Angels' jiggles and innuendo.

Charlie's Angels is now in re-run, but it's been replaced in the prime-time schedule by such programmes as *The A-Team*, which have even more jpm's. One episode of *The A-Team* included eight scenes in which guns were fired; six more scenes in which guns were flourished; four fist-fights; two car chases (one involving the chase of a taxiing plane through a jungle); two car crashes; four illegal acts committed by the team (one involving the sabotaging of a plane); eight acts of miscellaneous violence; one scene of sirens and flashing lights; four sudden noises (including a door being kicked in and a loudly dropped bowl of chicken soup); seven threats and five insults (mostly in jest among members of the team themselves). These fifty-one jolts resulted in only *one* person getting slightly hurt.

Now we have *Miami Vice*, a new kind of show, the rock video police programme. It uses rock selections by popular performers — such as the Rolling Stones — and combines them with tightly edited visual material. The result is television not unlike the videos one sees on *MuchMusic*. (The programme is simulcast on FM radio in a number of American cities.) And, as with rock videos, plot doesn't (and isn't supposed to) make sense. All that matters is the tension built up in the viewer through the beat of the music and the editing. The programme plays with the viewer's nervous system.

It's not just our imaginations telling us that programmes have speeded up in recent years and that there are far more jpm's on television now than there were in the 1950s and 1960s. Compare *Charlie's Angels* and *The A-Team* with *Dragnet*, an equally popular 1950s show in whose first sixty episodes a mere fifteen shots were fired. In those same sixty episodes, there was a total of three fights in which six punches were thrown. As Douglas Marshall of the Toronto *Star* put it in an obituary when Jack Webb died, "Nobody was ever in any doubt about the ingredients that made the *Dragnet* formula such a success: simple plots loosely based on real police files; gritty on-location realism; Friday's drab all-in-a-day's-work manner....All these elements contributed to an illusion of authenticity, the feeling that this was how it really was....By the end of the 1950s TV audiences had lost their innocence. One bullet every four episodes was no longer enough; they wanted fifteen jolts per minute."

I disagree with Marshall on the question of just when audiences began to crave more and more jpm's. With the exception of the *Untouchables*, TV didn't really speed up until 1968.* The programme that changed things was *Rowan & Martin's Laugh-In*, a show that suited the frenetic times in which it appeared. *Laugh-In* owed more to Amer-

---

* Even when *Dragnet* returned to the air in 1967 after an absence of seven years, it was still a slow-paced programme with even more emphasis on the policeman as someone who helps people. The new *Dragnet*, however, didn't last long.

ican film — the Keystone cops, the Marx Brothers, and Olsen & Johnson — than it did to television.* The programme consisted of a rapid series of short sketches, one-liners, blackouts, sight gags, catch phrases and cameo appearances by, among others, Richard Nixon. *Hee Haw* (1969) became country music's answer to *Laugh-In*. That programme, which is still on the air, specializes in atrocious one-liners delivered from the middle of a cornfield.

II

Sesame Street is another example of a popular American programme with high jpm content. The programme, which is seen by more than seventy-five per cent of North America's two-to-five-year-olds, became a hit as soon as it began in 1969. Like *Laugh-In* and *Hee Haw*, *Sesame Street* was unabashedly modelled on the staccato, fragmented style of a cluster of television commercials. "All art," Walter Pater wrote in the late nineteenth century, "constantly aspires toward the condition of music." In the late twentieth century, all television increasingly aspires to the condition of the TV commercial. *Sesame Street* consists of an average of forty-five items per hour — commercials for the letter Y, for the number 3, etc. The shortest items are five seconds long, the longest just over three minutes.

The programme is so popular that it can now be said, as it was of the old British Empire, that the sun never sets on *Sesame Street*. It's probably the most widely viewed (and celebrated) programme in the world. It's seen in almost sixty countries — in Brazil, in Indonesia, in Japan, in Pago

---

* In his essay "Americanitis" (1922), the great Russian film theorist Lev Kuleshov anticipates some of my argument. American films, he wrote, were the most appealing in the world. Their success lay "in the greatest common measure of film-ness, in the presence of maximum movement and in primitive heroism...."

Pago and in Zambia. Poland, Yugoslavia and Roumania show it, even mainland China has a version. There's a *Plaza Sesamo*, a *Vila Sesamo*, a *Via Sesame*, a *Rue Sesame*, a *Sesamstrasse*, a *Sesami Storito*, a *Sezamulica*. The children in McLuhan's global village are all watching *Sesame Street*.

But *Sesame Street* has its detractors. Mexican writer Guillermo Tenorio, for example, has criticized *Plaza Sesamo* as an "imperialist intrusion" into the social, educational and political life of countries where it's shown. In Britain, the BBC has refused to show *Sesame Street*. The BBC's head of children's programming asked, "Do we really have to import commercial hard-sell techniques into Britain because...American children will not watch anything quiet or thoughtful?" Concern has been expressed in New Zealand about how loud and aggressive the Muppets are. Others have criticized the programme's "violence," which they see as typically American. Undesirable characters are crushed under the weight of huge objects; letters get smashed or kicked off the screen. (Compared, of course, to the brutal violence of *Tom and Jerry*, *Road Runner* and other Saturday morning cartoons, *Sesame Street* is relatively tame.)

I spent many pleasant hours watching *Sesame Street* with my children when they were young. Now I sometimes still watch it alone. There's no doubt about the programme's entertainment value — each item is as beautifully crafted as the best-made commercials. But I do have doubts about its educational value. *Sesame Street*, after all, was originally intended to prepare children to read — to teach them "reading readiness." Research has shown that not just underprivileged children (for whom the show was originally intended), but all two-to-five-year-olds who watch *Sesame Street* know the names of the letters of the alphabet and the numbers from 1 to 20 better than those who don't watch the programme. Given *Sesame Street*'s constant repetition of that information, it would be astonishing if they didn't. The result is that more children enter school these days with the alphabet more firmly fixed in their heads than ever before.

But knowing the alphabet doesn't make one literate, any more than knowing the names of tools makes one a carpenter. I find it hard to believe that *Sesame Street* prepares children to read. Books, after all, have static printed pages and a very slow pace. *Sesame Street* has neither. I would argue that what the programme teaches is not a love of books, but a love of high jpm television. One doesn't graduate from *Sesame Street* to reading Victorian novels. On the contrary, I suspect one graduates from *Sesame Street* to watching high jpm programmes like *The A-Team* and rock videos. I'm not surprised to learn, therefore, that research has shown the *least* popular segments on *Sesame Street* are those in which books appear. And my guess is that if graduates of *Sesame Street* do read, they're far more likely to read print analogues of high jpm television — newspapers like the Edmonton or Toronto *Sun*, weekly magazines like *People* and *The National Enquirer*, and novels by writers like Judith Krantz (*Princess Daisy*). As George Gerbner of the Annenberg School of Communications puts it, television now "precedes reading and, increasingly, pre-empts it" for almost all children.

None of what I've said is meant to suggest that high jpm television programmes impair viewer intelligence. What I am suggesting is that a steady diet of nothing *but* high jpm television tends to condition viewer's nervous systems to respond only to a certain kind of stimulation. Their boredom thresholds are frequently so low that TV viewers find it difficult to enjoy anything that isn't fast-paced. Many of my film history students at the Ontario College of Art find the work of such directors as Carl Dreyer (*The Passion of Joan of Arc*) and Yasujiro Ozu (*Tokyo*

Story) too slow-paced for sensibilities conditioned by American television.

I have other reservations about *Sesame Street*, especially about some of the invisible lessons it teaches. The programme is sexist; seventy-five per cent of the cartoon and Muppet characters are male. Other invisible lessons include the notion that learning is an activity grown-ups initiate and control and that children are passive participants in; that one never goes off on tangents; and — now that stores everywhere carry a stock of *Sesame Street* products — that everyone has something to sell.

Many countries buy the right to show *Sesame Street*. Underdeveloped countries get it free. In Canada, although the CBC English network continued to produce two other daily programmes for children — *Mr. Dressup* and *The Friendly Giant* — it seemed clear from the amount of money the network lavished on Canadianizing *Sesame Street* that *it* is the cornerstone of CBC English-language programming for pre-schoolers. The CRTC encouraged that view when it waived its content regulations so *Sesame Street* counts as a *Canadian* programme. By arrangement with the Children's Television Workshop in New York (which produces *Sesame Street*), the CBC is permitted to replace the Spanish items of the American version with French items and to insert other items about the cultural and physical diversity of Canada — Raffi singing some of his hit children's songs, Beau Beaver's facts about Canada, metric segments. That material now adds up to twenty minutes per hour. The Children's Television Workshop doesn't permit the CBC to use puppets. All the number and letter sequences must be taken from the American show with the exception of the letter Z. The CBC may delete as many "zees" as it can and substitute "zeds." At one point, there was even talk of giving the CBC version a nice continentalist title of its own — *Sesame Street North*.

III

The actual content of American programmes doesn't matter much any more. Whether it's *The A-Team* or *Sesame Street*, it's only the structure, the number of jpm's, that counts. The result is that most programmes look more and more alike. As Ken Sobol put it in a submission to the Ontario Royal Commission on Violence in the Communications Industry, "The problem with this technique is that with it, violence becomes a structural rather than a story element. It's there automatically, before the story, not as a result of it. It becomes what we could call producer imposed violence, existing purely as a means of giving the audience a quick jolt, in hopes of keeping it interested until the next jolt. It is violence directed...against the nervous system of the viewer."

The kinds of jolts that are fashionable vary from one TV season to another. Insults — about twenty-five per half hour — are the basic building-blocks of sitcoms like *All in the Family* and *The Jeffersons*. Sex provides the jolts on other shows; we get the jiggling breasts and double entendres of *Three's Company* and *Three's A Crowd*. More recently we've had a number of programmes that one writer has described as "schlock-umentaries" — *Real People, More Real People, That's Incredible* — programmes that are a kind of cross between freak shows and the peeping-tomism of Allen Funt's *Candid Camera*. Much of the time what these shows do is provide the voyeurs in us with the ultimate in consumerism — we consume each other. It's video exhibitionism.

It's difficult to write quickly enough to get down all the items on thirty minutes of *Entertainment Tonight* (*E.T.*), TV's showbusiness magazine. On a typical episode we learn, among other things, that Bruce Springsteen is getting maiiied; Phil Collins is Number 1 on the pop charts; Martina Navratilova believes in aid to Africa, Dolph Sweet of *Gimme A Break* is dead of cancer; Edmund O'Brien is dead of Alzheimer's disease; far more people believe TV news than news from any other source; commercials are the leading source of product information in the U.S.; Carrie Fisher is in drug rehabilitation; Bette Davis's lawyers are thinking of suing her daughter; Eddie Murphy is going to appear in a Neil Simon comedy; Sharon Gless of *Cagney and Lacey* is about to make a TV movie with John Ritter; Clint Eastwood may work for Steven Spielberg; Tim Berringer is starring in a western spoof that calls for fourteen changes of costume and sixteen hats; Barbara Streisand is to star in the biography of a photographer; *Diff'rent Strokes* may not be the same when it switches to ABC; Burt Reynolds's house is for sale; Bette Midler is to play Mae West; American TV shows in Portugal are subtitled rather than dubbed; Peter Yarrow has rewritten "Puff the Magic Dragon" for the Cancer Society; Irving Berlin is ninety-seven.

When no one programme on the screen satisfies our restless craving for jpm's, we can always create our own with the help of the remote-control, push-button channel changers most of us now have. (I'll never forget how pleased I was when in the mid-1970s I first discovered the joy to be had from as simple an act as intercutting a Gerald Ford news conference with *Sesame Street*.) Some of us, I suspect, keep pushing the buttons because we're afraid we're going to miss something important if we don't.

Channel changers, says Gary Michael Dault, "make anthologists of us all, subdividing our seconds of viewing and logging our impatience-times as we scan the channels in search of something adhesive. In the time it takes an actor to shake a sack of dry dog food into a bowl, I've had a hectic glissando up and down and across the channels,...filling in the fore and aft parts of whatever I'm skipping over in an orgy of pattern recognition, reconstituting a language of which I hear only random syllables and (if I'm at the top of my form) phonemes in one long exuberant whoop of Orwellian Newspeak joy for our electric times."

Technology is making progress in other ways too. One American company, Emotional Response Index System Co. (ERIS), already uses computers to evaluate the popular appeal of scripts. I suspect it's just a matter of time until the producers of American programmes won't even have to bother with writers at all. It will be simpler to programme computers to turn out scripts designed to appeal to the greatest number of demographically correct viewers. After all, that's how the popular music that diverts the masses in the Oceania of *1984* was written.

In brief, the basic building-block of American commercial television is the jolt. There are visual, auditory and emotional jolts. There are jolts of information and jolts of laughter. Now there are even machines to help create jolts, such as Quantel, which inserts tiny pictures in various parts of the screen, zooms them up to full screen, and then back down again. As we'll see in the next two chapters, there are far more jpm's on American commercial television than on Canadian public TV.

The Canadian Oasis

I

Let's now add Canadian television to the picture I've been drawing. Compare the pace and tone of *Sesame Street* with that of two Canadian children's programmes that appear on the English-language network of the CBC every week-day morning — *The Friendly Giant* and *Mr. Dressup*.

The Friendly Giant, which has now unfortunately been reduced to re-runs and is soon to disappear, is a gentle, slow-paced, low-budget programme that has been on the network for twenty-six years. The unabashed purpose of this fifteen-minute show is to teach children a love of books and music. And there can be little doubt that it succeeds. Every morning the Friendly Giant, Bob Homme, invites us into the castle where he lives with his puppet friends, Rusty and Jerome. Sometimes Friendly reads a book, and as he does so the camera focuses lovingly on the static printed pages and their illustrations. Rusty and Jerome comment on the story in progress. (Good, reasonable conversation is another of *The Friendly Giant*'s components.) Sometimes we get a concert in which everyone in the castle makes music. Friendly plays the recorder, an instrument almost any young child can learn to play. The music is varied, ranging from madrigals to Cole Porter, from Bach to folk music and jazz.

Everything in Friendly's castle happens at the speed — and with the matter-of-factness — of everyday life. None of the frenetic pace of *Sesame Street* is found here. The little rituals that are part of *The Friendly Giant* never cease to affect me, no matter how many times I see and hear them. Friendly saying, "Once upon a time, not long ago and not far away," or "Look up. Look *way* up," after we're sitting in our cosy chairs by the fire. And there's always something bittersweet about leaving the castle and watching the drawbridge slowly go up as Friendly plays "Early One Morning."

Mr. Dressup is an equally slow-paced, low-budget programme. Ernie Coombes as Mr. Dressup, the puppet Casey, who represents a four-and-a-half-year-old, and their guests, show children how to make their own fun out of the odds and ends one finds around any house. Children watching the half-hour programme are encouraged to rely on themselves and take part in the activities, which can often continue long after the programme has ended. (*Sesame Street*, by contrast, invites a far more passive involvement on the part of its viewers.) And *Mr. Dressup*, like *The Friendly Giant*, assumes that children have an attention span that extends beyond two minutes, an assumption that's reflected in the structure, style and content of both programmes. The average minute of *Sesame Street* contains a minimum of ten edits, compared to three or four on *Mr. Dressup* and *The Friendly Giant*. When it was announced that *The Friendly Giant* had been cancelled, one mother wrote the Toronto *Star* to say that it "is the only television show that can hold the attention of my fifteen-month-old son for longer than thirty seconds at a time. In fact, much to my amazement, he sits himself on the couch and remains there, mesmerized, for the entire fifteen minutes, and it is only upon hearing the closing theme that he resumes his usual ransacking of the living room."

Like Rusty and Jerome on *The Friendly Giant*, Casey participates as an equal with Mr. Dressup. Sometimes he initiates things and, like real children, his curiosity can often take him off on tangents. That's all right with Mr. Dressup. (One never goes off on tangents on *Sesame Street*.) The puppets on both *Mr. Dressup* and *The Friendly Giant* have the kind of crummy homemade look of puppets that real kids might make for themselves. (*Sesame Street* wouldn't be caught dead with such puppets.)

There are a number of other Canadian television programmes for young children, both on the CBC and on the educational networks of the provinces, that (with one exception) are unlike anything found on American TV. (The exception, of course, is *Mister Rogers' Neighbourhood* on PBS. My own children never took to Mr. Rogers; they found him patronizing.) *Polka Dot Door*, for example, a slow-paced programme on TVO, the Ontario educational network, is very much in the tradition of *Mr. Dressup* and *The Friendly Giant*. It emphasizes games and activities children can participate in at home; every day there's a book to read and songs. *Passe-Partout*, on the Quebec network, and *Size Small* in Saskatchewan are similar programmes. Also on TVO is a British show called *Vision On*, which encourages children to use readily available materials to make art. Viewers send in examples of their work, and one often sees startlingly creative pieces by very young children.

And some important independent productions for children are now being done in association with the CBC. *The Kids of DeGrassi Street* is a series about the realistic adventures of a group of inner-city children in Toronto. *The Elephant Show*, with popular recording stars Sharon, Lois and Bram, is a weekly half-hour of songs, games and dances from around the world. (One of the effects of good Canadian children's programming on TV has been a growing market for quality Canadian books and records for children.)

Fraggle Rock is a Canadian-American co-production. I realize I'm in a minority, but I find it too calculatedly cute. And its deliberate cultural ambiguity bothers me. It pretends to be from everywhere and nowhere at the same time. Unlike his books, there's nothing Canadian about Dennis Lee's *Fraggle Rock* lyrics. "[We make] it look as if it were produced in the country that's seeing it," says Jim Henson's director of international production. "It doesn't look racially specific." But that's the trouble. I would much prefer that the CBC used its limited resources, financial and otherwise, to produce distinctively *Canadian* children's programmes. Certainly, we've shown that we can do so.

II

What's My Line, the longest-running game show in the history of prime-time American television, first appeared on CBS in 1950 and ran until 1967. But there's no way *What's My Line* could be considered for prime-time television today. It had too few jpm's — no flashing lights, no screaming audience, no smart-ass host. Contestants on the show were asked simple yes or no questions by four panelists who tried to guess what (usually off-beat) job the contestant had. Each time a contestant said no, he or she got *five* dollars; ten no's ended the game. That's all there was to it.

And if what we sometimes got on flashier American game shows of the 1950s — shows such as *The $64,000 Question* — were *idiots savants*, people who knew everything about one subject and nothing about anything else,*

---

* Teddy Nadler, a clerk from St. Louis with a photographic memory, had memorized a whole encyclopedia. In 1958, he won $252,000 on *The $64,000 Challenge*, the most anyone has ever won on a TV game show. Two years later, Nadler failed a test to become a census taker because he didn't know the difference between east and west.

what we have on today's game shows — *The Price is Right*, etc. — are genial fools, people who don't seem to know much about anything, but who look so pleasant and seem so nice that it would be mean-spirited to expect them to be intelligent too. (Smart-ass male host: "Tell us about yourself, Mary Lou." Contestant: "I'm twenty-three. I like people, animals, plants and colours. My favourite one is pink." Loud applause.) On these game shows, the host, his sexy female assistants, and the audience of other genial fools all play the part of cheerleaders for the consumer society; they jump up and down and shout wildly as piles of consumer goods are displayed, caressed and given away to those who know how many times Elizabeth Taylor and Debbie Reynolds have been married.

In 1957, the CBC decided to attempt to break the stranglehold that *What's My Line*, *The $64,000 Question* and other prime-time American game shows had on Canadian audiences. *Front Page Challenge* was the result. The word "Challenge" in the title was borrowed from *The $64,000 Challenge*. (It has a kind of American, free-enterprise ring to it.) *Front Page Challenge* tried to be American in other ways too. On the first few shows, beautiful models escorted guests to their places; there were clocks and buzzers and flashing lights; there were also more guests than there are today, which made the pace of the programme faster than it is now.

Today *Front Page Challenge* is the only prime-time, network programme in North America that is dominated by men and women over the age of sixty. On most other programmes, older people either don't exist or exist merely as objects of derision. Certainly one sees comparatively few people over the age of thirty on American game shows. As Jonathan Goodson, producer of *Card Sharks*, puts it, "If there's an unwritten law that you have to be young and beautiful to be on American game shows, God wrote it."

The game the panel plays on *Front Page Challenge* is both entertaining and informative. The identification of a news story provides an excuse for what the programme is really about, the discussion of some current issue with a prominent newsmaker. The same thing is true of *Fighting Words*, both in its original incarnation with Nathan Cohen as host and in its new version with Peter Gzowski: the identification of the author of a quotation provides an excuse for intelligent, opinionated people to debate the merits of the quotation.

III

By the time the CBC came on the air in 1952, the Americans had been producing TV programmes for several years. Naturally, the CBC looked to the U.S. for know-how in a number of programme areas. American producers taught Canada's first TV clergymen how to sit in front of a camera and how to hold a Bible as effectively as announcers displayed soap and other products. They taught altar attendants *not* to polish church brass because it would glint and create black spots on the television screen.

In the U.S., TV religion came to be dominated by fundamentalism, a largely American phenomenon that began at the turn of the century as a reaction against Darwinism. The battle between those two forces culminated in the famous Scopes trial of 1925, after which fundamentalism retreated from the national scene for almost thirty years. In the 1950s, Billy Graham made brilliant use of television and revived the movement. He carefully avoided the controversial issues that had tripped up his predecessors. Graham focused instead on a simple, compelling appeal to individual sinners — to anyone who felt guilty about virtually anything — to be reborn in Christ.

Other fundamentalist preachers soon joined Graham on American (and, therefore, on Canadian) television screens. Men with names that Hollywood couldn't have improved on: Oral Roberts, Rex Humbard, Jerry Falwell, Jimmy Swaggart and, my favourite, Ernest Angley (pronounced Angel-y). Angley comes to us from Akron, Ohio, and with his beady eyes and pasty complexion, he looks like a kind of born-again Frankenstein monster. There's something both cuddly and sinister about him. He tells us, with a weird smile, that he was "born to win the lost at any cost." He talks tearfully of his own suffering — especially of the death of his wife, Angel. Angel Angley. His life-size hand appears on the the television screen, and he invites us to reach out and make contact with his screen hand. (In the days before TV, Oral Roberts used to tell us to put our hands on our radios.) Angley urges us to pick up our spiritual phones and dial F-A-I-T-H. There's no other way, he says, to get rid of our "spiritual fleas" and gain "cope power." *"Out, thou nicotine spirit!"* he shouts at a self-confessed cigarette smoker who stands trembling before him. Then he straight-arms her in the face (at least that's what it looks like) and she falls into the arms of two men who look like ex-football players, and whose job it is to catch fallen sinners.

Angley, like Oral Roberts, Rex Humbard and Jerry Falwell, appears once a week. But in recent years, other American fundamentalists have developed a new kind of religious programme — the daily Christian talk show. The most prominent of these shows — *PTL* (People That Love) with hosts Jim and Tammy Bakker (pronounced Baker) and *The 700 Club* with Pat Robertson — are seen widely in Canada and the U.S. These programmes buy time, usually in the early morning or late evening, when sad and lonely people are watching (and the rates are cheap). Paid religion has given many independent stations and network affiliates a whole new source of income.

The Bakkers, Pat Robertson and their guests — fundamentalists and born-again Christians like Pat Boone and Charles Colson — smile a lot and are fond of saying things like "Praise the Lord" and "Thank you, Jesus." Every so often we're told about sinners who have called in to say they've been saved. Sometimes we're shown film clips of those who've been saved. Guests and hosts frequently join hands to pray for homosexuals and other sinners — those who play "Dungeons and Dragons," for instance. Always implicit is the assumption that once you've become a born-again Christian your troubles are over.

In the early 1970s the Committee for an Independent Canada complained to the CRTC about U.S. domination of religious programming seen in Canada. (Under twenty per cent of the programmes seen here were actually being produced in Canada.) Pierre Juneau, then head of the CRTC, agreed that more *Canadian* religious programmes were needed. Two groups came to the rescue. Canada's largest evangelical congregation, The People's Church of Toronto, converted its main hall into a television studio. Its pastor, Paul Smith, decided that *he* would compete every Sunday with the likes of Jerry Falwell, Oral Roberts and Rex Humbard. Then along came *100 Huntley Street*, a daily Christian talk show with perhaps the most earnest of all TV preachers, David Mainse, as host. *People's Church* and *100 Huntley Street* are less strident, more soft sell than their American counterparts. But when Zenon Andrusyshyn, former kicker for the Toronto Argonauts, appears on *100 Huntley Street*, he looks and sounds just like the born-again athletes we see on *PTL* and *The 700 Club*.

A visitor from another galaxy looking at all these religious programmes might conclude that religion and reasonableness on the planet Earth are mutually exclusive. But there is in fact a religious programme — the CBC's *Man Alive* with host Roy Bonisteel — that disproves that notion. For more than fifteen years now, in a quiet, thoughtful way (and in prime time), *Man Alive* has examined some of the more thorny ethical and moral questions of our time with an honesty that's rare. There's nothing like it on American television. In a programme on homosexuality and the church, *Man Alive* presented a profoundly moving interview with a Roman Catholic priest who, although celibate, regarded himself as a homosexual. His church, he said, had been of no help to him in coming to terms with his sexuality.

Man Alive takes its name from the work of a second-century bishop, St. Irenaeus, for whom "the glory of God is man fully alive." Being fully alive, for the producers of this programme, has meant pushing themselves, and us, to be as aware, concerned and committed as possible. That's a great deal more than one can say about most of the religious programming to be found elsewhere on television. And it's interesting to note that the proposed religious Pay-TV network is not evangelical, but arises from the social justice, ecumenical tradition of Canada's mainstream churches.

IV

I've travelled widely in Canada over the past decade, and I've made a point of watching the local news everywhere I've been. And everywhere I've seen a striking difference between the local news on Canadian channels and that on American channels. With the exception of CITY-TV in Toronto (which I discuss in chapter 4), American local newscasts have far more jpm's. There's a much greater emphasis on fires, burglaries, murders, on sensational items of all kinds. These items are frequently accompanied by as much "eyewitness" footage as possible — we see lots of flashing lights, stretchers and, wherever possible, blood. Grieving family members often have microphones shoved in their faces. The announcers on American local news shows tend to speak more quickly; their prose is more dramatic.

There's little difference in structure, on the other hand, between the CBC's *The National* and the 6:30 p.m. newscasts of the three commercial American networks. The CBC, NBC, ABC and CBS have all clearly learned a great deal from *Sesame Street* about how to reduce complicated issues to fast-moving, one-to-two-minute items, how to make the news sound and look as slick as a commercial. ABC's *World News Tonight*, in particular, has been criticized for its showbiz approach — for illuminating the entire front of a Viennese cathedral, for example, in order to provide a backdrop for a news item. "Why not?" asked the programme's executive producer. "It may not mean much in the book of life, but it made a pretty shot." And, unfortunately, pretty shots are of crucial importance. That fact, as Peter Trueman says in *Smoke & Mirrors*, "puts undue emphasis on the abnormal. Normal is dull, and unlike a newspaper, which is not intended to be read cover to cover, television cannot afford dull patches. Too many of those drive the viewer to change channels or shut the set off completely."

Like American network newscasts, *The National* relies on its reporters' ability to reduce complicated issues to fast-moving, tightly edited, visual essays with a simple narrative structure and wide audience appeal. Thus TV news stories are more persuasive than newspaper stories.

No one has been more effective at using this form in the past couple of years than Brian Stewart in his moving reports from drought-stricken Africa. But there are dangers involved. In *The Powers That Be*, David Halberstam laments the extent to which TV has speeded up everything. "Every event, every personality, every fad," he writes, "comes and goes at an ever accelerating rate." The drought continues, but it no longer makes the news.

The National may not be different in structure but it is different in two important ways. Unlike its American counterparts, it's now broadcast at 10 p.m. — in prime time. And it's followed by *The Journal*, a programme which takes an in-depth look at some of the items on the news. By moving *The National* to 10 p.m. and adding *The Journal*, the CBC has stated clearly that it regards its mandate to inform Canada about itself and the rest of the world to be of prime importance. Unfortunately, *The National* still isn't as Canadian in its international coverage as it might be. It has far too few reporters abroad. For example, there's no one covering South or Central America. The result is that too much of the news footage we see from these places isn't Canadian.

But there can be no doubt that *The National* is the best front page in Canada. There's no better place to go (other than perhaps CBC radio's *The World At Six* or Radio-Canada's *Téléjournal*) to get a fast overview of the most important stories of the day. But *The National* obviously can't offer the range of opinion and analysis we need to be reasonably well-informed. One can't follow as complicated a story as Lebanon just by watching *The National*. We need newspapers, magazines and books — and Canadian current affairs shows, like *the fifth estate* and *Canada AM*. There's often material of interest as well on such American programmes as ABC's *Nightline*, CBS's *Nightwatch*, and PBS's *The MacNeil/Lehrer Report* and *Washing-*

ton Week in Review. Every weekday for over a decade, *As It Happens* has captured something of the energy and controversy of the world around us on radio. Now *The Journal* is attempting to do the same thing. And it's doing it well. Executive producer Mark Starowicz has brought off an enormously difficult assignment.

The Journal examines the news in two ways — through documentary reports, which tend to be very good, and through interviews, which are sometimes good and sometimes not. *The Journal*'s international documentaries — no one does more — are perhaps the best on North American TV. Nothing I've seen elsewhere compares with Ann Medina's reports from Lebanon, Nicaragua and India, or Peter Kent's reports from Poland and Cambodia. (Peter Kent is no longer with the CBC.) Background and factions are made remarkably clear. Unfortunately, there's no one on *The Journal* whose interviewing skills compare with those of the suberb Ted Koppel on ABC's *Nightline*, or with those of Patrick Watson on any number of CBC programmes. Barbara Frum, it seems to me, was better on radio's *As It Happens*, where editing could do more to help shape an interview. On television her facial expressions are often a distraction. And there's something too self-important about MaryLou Finlay as interviewer.

In addition to *The National* and *The Journal*, the CBC now brings us *Midday* from 12 to 1 p.m. weekdays. *Midday* consists of a brief newscast followed by interviews, background material and columnists' reports which makes for a lively and intelligent programme.

V

Public affairs programmes on television frequently do little more than repeat material we've already read in newspapers and magazines. That's unfortunate, since at their best the print media and television can reinforce one another. Print is good at providing factual information, television at offering impressions, at filling in the spaces around the words. Print can give us the thoughts of Tom Berger; a programme such as *90 Minutes Live* gives us the man. The well-informed citizen needs both.

The fifth estate, which has been on the air since 1975, is probably the best weekly public affairs show we've had on Canadian television. Unlike CTV's *W5*, *the fifth estate* doesn't just repeat newspaper and magazine stories. Unlike one of its own predecessors, *This Hour Has Seven Days*, and CBS's *60 Minutes*, it avoids sensationalizing issues. What the programme does over and over again is tell us that the world is far less predictable, far more complicated than most of us would like to think. If *W5* or *60 Minutes* had done an item on Mormon Alex Joseph and his eleven wives (Joseph added a twelfth wife during *the fifth estate*'s filming), it would have had a predictable, patronizing tone to it. After all, there are a lot of freaks, crazies and true believers out there. One of the easiest ways to fill sixty minutes of television time (and draw large audiences) is by showing us as many of those people as possible, which is what programmes like *Real People* specialize in. But what *the fifth estate* presented in that programme was a gentle, articulate man and twelve bright, attractive women (one of whom holds a law degree) who've chosen to live together and seem happy with the arrangement. When *the fifth estate* deals with matters that *are* in the news, it almost always does so in a way that offers fresh information and insight. Nothing I read came even close to doing as good a job of putting the racial nuances of the enormously complicated air traffic controllers' dispute of the mid-1970s into perspective. "Plane Language" won an ACTRA award as best programme of the year.

But what *the fifth estate* does best of all is original reporting; it creates headlines. Sometimes the programme gets
the credit it deserves; sometimes it doesn't. In November
1978, for example, *the fifth estate* broadcast a brilliant hour-
long item entitled "A Passage of Arms," which revealed
that weapons were being shipped from Saint John, N.B.,
to South Africa via Antigua by a company known as the
Space Research Corporation (SRC), despite a 1963 U.N.
embargo on such shipments. With the help of Canada
and Israel, among other countries, South Africa had in
a short time transformed its small army into one of the
ten most powerful armies in the world. *The fifth estate*
expected "A Passage of Arms" would result in a public
furor. But there was little reaction. Canadian newspapers
didn't carry the story or they pooh-poohed it. The Toronto
Star dismissed the item, saying that an RCMP investiga-
tion into the matter had disclosed nothing.

The fifth estate continued to pursue the story. In January
1980, it presented an update which revealed that SRC
had been given a $1 million grant by the Department of
Trade, Industry and Commerce to promote its products
abroad. *The fifth estate* item also told us that it had learned
that the Department of Justice had been sitting for some
time on an RCMP file recommending prosecution of SRC.
Again newspapers dismissed the story. "Arms firm
complains of CBC harassment," declared an Ottawa *Journal* headline. Gerald Bull, head of SRC, told the paper
he'd been getting calls from *the fifth estate* and he didn't
like it.

Early in March 1980, fifteen months after *the fifth estate*
first broke the story, the *Globe and Mail* published a four-
part series, "Apartheid Arms Probe," by investigative
reporter Peter Moon. Apart from an interview with "a
senior SRC official" (Bull himself?), Moon's articles did
nothing to further the story *the fifth estate* had told us.

They just tidied it up a bit. Moon admits he'd screened the show and had interviewed its producer (Bill Cran) at length. Yet nowhere in this four-part series did he or the *Globe and Mail* acknowledge that *the fifth estate* and the CBC had had anything to do with the story. (I assume this is because of the rivalry between the two media.) Later that March, the *Globe* reported in a front-page story that Gerald Bull, president of the SRC, had pleaded guilty to a charge of illegally shipping arms through Canada to South Africa. Again, *the fifth estate*'s crucial role in uncovering the story wasn't mentioned. Perhaps the most remarkable thing about this item is that it's not inherently a visual story. That didn't keep *the fifth estate* from pursuing it.

The fifth estate does have its flaws. The title itself is pretentious. The notion that the fourth estate — the press — needs to be distinguished from a fifth estate — television — seems silly: a reporter is a reporter, with or without a camera. (And if you come right down to it, the use of the term "estate" is meaningless in a democratic society. Representation by estates was replaced by representation by population some time ago.)

There are no hour-long items on CBS's *60 Minutes*. Each episode consists of three or four slickly packaged items. As *Time* magazine puts it, "the show has elements of high melodrama: most of its investigative pieces are playlets in which a Lone Ranger journalist corners a villain, not with a gun but with an interview." Real life confrontations, unfortunately, are rarely so neat. Many of the profiles on *60 Minutes* are right out of the pages of *People* magazine. An item on Bette Davis, for instance, focuses on her four marriages and two abortions — not on her philosophy of acting. Denise Bombardier of Radio Canada's *Le Point* has expressed concern about the "lack of intellectual content in television journalism. People rave about *60 Minutes*," she says, "but as far as I'm concerned, that style of investigative journalism is nothing more than sophisticated gossip."

Is it any wonder, then, that the high jpm *60 Minutes* has been one of the most popular American shows in recent years, right up there with *The A-Team*? *60 Minutes*, I would argue, probably more than any other programme, is responsible for our having become what I call "infomaniacs." We're terrified of war, convinced the world around us is out of control. But we don't turn to serious newspapers and magazines — we don't have the attention spans for that. Instead, like ravenous Pac-men, we gobble up more and more TV news. Newzak. And the amount available seems to be increasing. I know people who keep the American Cable News Network on in the background all the time. Such programmes reassure us for the moment. Our need for order and meaning, says anthropologist Cliffort Geertz, is "as real and pressing as the more familiar biological needs." We feel that if Mike Wallace or whoever is looking into it, everything is OK. Each item is structured to provide us with the kind of "sweet resolution of anxiety" we get when our football team wins. (That lovely phrase comes from a CBS executive.) The fact that the next day we can't remember a word of what was said is irrelevant.

The Economic Council of Canada has described the process this way: "The successful journalist must take the raw ingredients — the issues of, and the actors in, the decision-making process — and by chopping, grinding, mashing, blending, baking, boiling and frying, convert them into attractive food for the average palate." On the receiving end, "The vast majority of viewers/listeners/readers want all things on their information menu to be black or white, true or false, good or bad — preferably seasoned with a pinch of sensationalism and intimate personal detail of the famous, and served on a platter of conventional belief."

VI

Sometimes, as we've seen, the CBC is successful at taking an American form — such as the game show — and giving it a distinctly Canadian flavour. Sometimes the CBC is less successful, as in the case of its attempt to develop a late-night talk show to compete with Johnny Carson, Dick Cavett and Merv Griffin.

Many of us assume that popular television shows are easy to produce. Most of them are so mindless, they've got to be easy. It's disconcerting to discover that most TV programmes — including the trashiest — are difficult to do. People who can readily accept the fact that it took the Toronto Blue Jays several years to get to be good at baseball somehow expect a programme like *90 Minutes Live* and host Peter Gzowski to be terrific first time out. We forget that Gzowski was lousy at first on radio — much too acerbic. It took him a long time to lose that tone. Even *This Country in the Morning*, excellent radio programme that it was, didn't really take off immediately. The success of *As It Happens* was longer in the making. We forget that *This Hour Has Seven Days* took a year to hit its stride. So did *the fifth estate*. And there were a lot of bad episodes of *King of Kensington* before we had some good ones.

What was important about each of these programmes was that there was something essentially right about them that made their ultimate success worth waiting for. I'm one of a small minority who believe that was also true of *90 Minutes Live*. Unfortunately, CBC's executives wouldn't wait and cancelled the programme. Certainly the list of things that were wrong with Gzowski and the show was a long one. Gzowski was slow at learning the business of television — knowing what camera to look at, how to take cues, how to remember all the things one needs to remember to get through an evening and still look comfortable. He wasn't loose enough to ride with an interview that was deviating from the path his staff had prepared him for, or loose enough to change the plan of the programme if someone or something came along that deserved more time. If Gzowski was too acerbic at first on radio, he was too genial on TV. His almost perpetual grin caused one reviewer to suggest that Gzowski seemed to be suffering from terminal euphoria. The world may not have been quite ready for the rumpled, sad-faced, off-camera Gzowski who swears a lot and looks as if he's just come from taking a spin in a clothes dryer, but the slick Gzowski was too much. That was the show's biggest mistake — one that could and should have been corrected.

There were other mistakes. Out of what I assume was a desire to keep things moving so viewers wouldn't get bored, there were often too many guests on the programme. That frequently resulted in a sense of missed opportunities. If you're going to bring on Edgar Z. Friedenberg, you've got to give him enough time to say something. And there were mistakes in booking. A guy who blew himself up in a coffin with six sticks of dynamite may have been the ultimate in jpm's, but I think we could have managed without him. And I don't know what the point is of having Maureen Forrester sing popular songs badly when there are tens of thousands who've never had the chance to hear her sing a Mahler *lied*.

Despite these problems, there was a great deal that was good and distinctive about *90 Minutes Live*. I liked the absence of people "known for their well-knownness" — people like Fernando Lamas and Zsa Zsa Gabor who abound on American talk shows. Those of the show's guests known for their well-knownness tended to be there for a good reason. Nothing I'd read about or by Timothy Leary was quite as revealing of the shallowness of the man as his appearance on *90 Minutes Live*.

The show introduced me to a lot of interesting Canadians: Mayor Stephen Juba of Winnipeg who spent $20,000 a year of his own money feeding Winnipeg's birds. Humphrey and the Dump Trucks, a good folk-rock group from Saskatchewan. Maria Campbell, a haunting half-breed. There were other memorable moments too. John Candy getting a man in a Burnaby, B.C., shopping centre to gift wrap some moose antlers. Four young men from Tuktoyaktuk and Inuvik illustrating events from the Northern Games. Richard Monette doing a wonderful bit from Michel Tremblay's *Hosanna*. Mordecai Richler (who turns out to be a very shy man) awkwardly revealing that he'd never heard of Anne Murray.

Peter Gzowski was roasted by viewers, critics and colleagues within the CBC because he wasn't Johnny Carson. Any fool could see that Gzowski wasn't Carson. But in focusing on what Gzowski *wasn't*, most viewers failed to see that he and his show were making an important contribution to our understanding of Canadian life. We still need a late-night show on the CBC English network.

VII

Before I turn to the various kinds of dramatic programme offered by the CBC in the next chapter, I'd like to touch briefly on two more information shows that appear weekly on the English-language network — *Marketplace* and *The Nature of Things*.

There's no comparison between the high jpm American consumer programme *Fight Back!* and the CBC's *Marketplace*. *Fight Back!* is pure showbiz. Fast-talking host David Horowitz looks more like the late Andy Kaufman doing a comic routine than he does a consumer advisor. An item on the value of aerobic exercise is filled with jiggling women. We're teased about whether a car can travel 190 miles on four gallons of gas as advertised. A studio audience cheers Horowitz on. As a friend put it, this isn't a TV version of *Consumer Reports*; it's *Consumer Revenge.*

And there is nothing on American commercial television to compare with *The Nature of Things*, a weekly, prime-time CBC programme about the world of science.* *The Nature of Things* isn't able to deal with nearly the range of subjects that the CBC's radio programme, *Quirks and Quarks*, can. How does one make a math item or a chemistry item interesting? But as host David Suzuki's recent eight-part mini-series, *A Planet for the Taking*, revealed, *The Nature of Things can* deal with ideas and deal with them well. In *A Planet for the Taking*, Suzuki questions western man's anthropocentric view of the universe, the notion that somehow the world of nature exists to be tamed by man. Science, he says, has now come to regard death not as a normal part of life, but as the ultimate enemy to be overcome. The arrogance of that view, he suggests, leads to considerable folly.

In contrast with most science and nature shows which simply offer us breathtaking views of things, *The Nature of Things*, in the tradition of CBC's other public affairs shows, is frequently controversial. In a 1984 show called "The Great Lakes and Troubled Waters", for example, Dr. Ross Hall, a biochemist at McMaster University and an expert on water quality in the Great Lakes, stated, "We know we're dealing with toxic chemicals. We know they're getting into the drinking water. What we don't know is what...precise effect it has on you. And because we can't make the linkage, many of our public authorities...refuse

---

* There *are* science programmes, including *The Nature of Things*, on PBS.

to act because they can't see any connection. The linkage is there. It's fuzzy. It's not precise, but nevertheless it's there." The programme went on to point out that the same governments that claim to be waiting for precise data have cut back funding for research efforts that could produce the data. The only way to bring about change, *The Nature of Things* suggested, was through public pressure.

As we've seen in the preceding pages, non-dramatic programming on Canadian public television, most particularly on the CBC, is structurally different from American commerical television. Can we see the same difference in dramatic programming?

Dramatically Speaking

I

There's a lot of silliness in American soap opera (continuing drama) that requires a willing suspension of disbelief. Actors speak far more slowly than people normally do and with numerous pauses for dramatic effect. That's one of the ways emotional jolts are registered. Although there are more doctors per square foot in daytime soap operas than anywhere in the world, those who inhabit that world know nothing of contraception — the ratio of pregnancies to couplings is higher in soapland than anywhere on earth. So great is the risk that even women who've had hysterectomies become pregnant. Giving birth itself is more hazardous than going over Niagara Falls in a barrel. But what the doctors lose in miscarriages, stillbirths and dead mothers, they more than make up for in cancer cures, at which they seem to be the best in the world. Children who are lucky enough to survive the trauma of birth often disappear, only to reappear during custody battles and/or when they're old enough to start fooling around. Amnesia occurs in epidemic proportions. (One amnesiac on *The Days of Our Lives* went upstairs for a nap and didn't come down for two years.) There are almost no poor blacks. There's no unemployment. Everyone has impeccable taste. I've never seen a bad dresser on a soap. I've never seen a pimple.

One has to accept all these things — and more. Nonetheless, one can still argue that continuing drama offers *less* of an escape (is more real) than almost any other fiction regularly seen on American TV. If other television programmes perpetuate the notion that life consists of discrete problems that can be neatly wrapped up in thirty or sixty minute solutions, continuing drama tells us that life is a process consisting of never-ending problems and ever-changing relationships. One never arrives at a point at which there are easy answers. The church and the extended family used to teach these things; those institutions no longer exist for many of us. Now we get our instruction in the continuity of human existence from daily American television programmes like *All My Children* and *The Days of Our Lives*, and weekly shows such as *Dallas*. These shows, as Renata Adler has written, provide us with "the most steady, open-ended sadness to be found outside life itself." But even the soaps are changing. The pace of events has so speeded up in the last few years that the soaps have become increasingly implausible. *The Days of Our Lives*, for example, now resembles the serials of old-time Saturday matinees more than it does traditional soap opera. Characters we're certain are dead keep coming back to life.

There is currently no daily or weekly continuing drama on the CBC English-language network except the BBC's *Coronation Street*. The Craigs, the Plouffes and the Prides are long gone. (On French-Canadian television continuing drama flourishes on the *téléromans*.) Instead, what we've had in recent years are such serials (continuing dramas) as *A Gift to Last*, *Home Fires* and *Empire Inc. A Gift to Last*, a twenty-two part series spread over three seasons, told the story of the Sturgess family of Tamarack, Ontario, a town not far from Toronto. It's the turn of the century. Edgar Sturgess is a free spirit, but even free spirits have to grow up. Edgar (Gordon Pinsent) is eventually saddened into adulthood by the Boer War and the marriage of Sheila, the woman he loves, to another man. (At the end of the second season, Edgar and Sheila finally get together after Sheila's no-good husband is killed off.) *Home Fires*, a series that ran from the fall of 1980 to the fall of 1983, tells the story of a Toronto family, the Lowes, struggling to maintain some semblance of family life while the Second World War rages overseas. Every adult does everything he or she can to contribute to the war effort.

Rooted in the past, family dramas such as *A Gift to Last* and *Home Fires* not only teach us about the cycle of life, they also offer incidental instruction in social history. In *A Gift to Last*, for instance, one is struck, on the one hand, by the patriotic fervour with which these late Victorians sing "God Save The Queen" and, on the other, by their growing resentment of continuing British control of Canada's armed forces. One feels ashamed of the contempt English-Canadians have for French-Canadians. "This is a British country," says one woman, "and you can't have a Frenchman [Laurier] running it. It isn't natural." In *Home Fires*, Dr. Lowe is interned under the terms of the War Measures Act because he has left-wing sympathies. Young women old enough to join the armed forces still ask their fathers' permission to marry.

Empire Inc. was a comparatively short (six-part) family drama first seen in the fall of 1983. The show, which covers the years from 1924 to the 1960s, consciously tried to find a middle ground between the production values of such British serials as *Brideshead Revisited* and the popular appeal of such American melodramas as *Dallas*. To a large extent, *Empire Inc.* succeeded. Certainly it was far better written and performed than *Dallas*. And it was enormously successful in the ratings.

Like J.R. Ewing, James Munroe is an aggressive and ruthless businessman. But he's far more complicated than J.R. We know how J.R. is going to behave in almost any situation; we're much less certain about Munroe. Munroe, for example, is an insomniac haunted by a recurring nightmare about his betrayed partner's suicide. Like Orson Welles's Charles Foster Kane, he can put love ahead of personal advancement. When his disturbed daughter joins the Nazis, he refuses to dissociate himself from her, thereby ending his political career. If we despise the young Munroe, who has, among other things, manipulated his way into marriage to a socialite, we pity the old man who is powerless and alone.*

Like *A Gift to Last* and *Home Fires*, *Empire Inc.* is rooted in our culture and history without being heavy-handed about it. As producer Mark Blandford put it, "I'm all for doing work that explores Canadian roots, but roots are under the ground, not draped over the leaves." And unlike *A Gift to Last* and *Home Fires*, which concern themselves, as almost all Canadian drama does, with marginal characters, *Empire Inc.* deals with the powerful financial establishment of old Montreal. Munroe's career is reminiscent of the Bronfmans and Molsons.** And although French-English tension is a minor theme, one senses the stirrings of the Quiet Revolution in the background.

When John Meisel took over at the CRTC, he said Canadians needed their own versions of *Dallas* — popular, well-made TV shows with Canadian stars and themes that were entertaining enough to keep viewers tuned in. *Empire Inc.* was such a show.

---

* And there's Munroe's sense of irony. "They used to call me a robber baron," he says at one point. "Now I'm a much loved philanthropist....I think they call that public relations."

** Blandford told one reporter, "Although *Empire, Inc.* is pure entertainment, I also think that if a nation is to become intelligently conscious, it should try to understand how the powerful classes operate. The Scottish establishment of old financial Montreal, which was a closed community, and quite powerful in its day, provides that kind of context."

II

By the 1970s on U.S. television the documentary realism of police shows such as *Dragnet* had given way to the hyper-realism of *Kojak*, *The Streets of San Francisco* and *Starsky and Hutch*. (I deal with *Cagney and Lacey* and *Hill Street Blues* in the next chapter.) These new shows offered us a great deal of violence for the sake of violence, as policemen raced around the roughest parts of town, tires screeching and guns drawn, tackling pimps, pushers and the like.

Compare these American police shows with the realism of CBC's *Sidestreet*. The show, which ran in the mid-to-late 1970s, featured two Toronto policemen who spend much of their time preventing crime. In an episode titled *The Rebellion of Bertha Mackenzie*, for example, an Indian woman's welfare has been cut off by an overly rigid social worker. The woman's radical brother believes that Métis power is the only solution and he turns her home into an armed camp. The policemen, played by Donnelly Rhodes and Jonathan Welsh, defuse this potentially explosive situation, and do so without firing a shot. Like *Wojeck* in the late 1960s, a programme about a Toronto coroner, and *The Collaborators* in the early 1970s, a programme about two forensic scientists — like almost all serial drama on the CBC — *Sidestreet* was mostly about social issues. From watching American police shows, you can't imagine safely walking the streets of any large American city. In the Toronto of *Sidestreet*, as in the real Toronto, you can safely walk almost any place.

The Great Detective, a CBC police series of the early 1980s, is in the same documentary tradition as *The Collaborators*, *Wojeck* and *Sidestreet*. The story, set in late nineteenth-century Ontario, is loosely based on some of the adventures of the first — and for a long time, only — detective serving the province outside Toronto. Unfortunately, *The Great Detective* wasn't as well written as its predecessors, nor as well produced. Its scripts often left loose ends, and its frequently garbled lines suggested a budget with little money for retakes. But whatever its faults, there was no doubt the show was Canadian. As David Wesley of the Hamilton *Spectator* wrote, "Less pompously refined than British mysteries, and not as slick as U.S. detective series, it [had] all the rough hewn beauty of a piece of Canadian pine furniture."

III

From the time *The Plouffes* went off the air in 1959, the CBC assumed that the Americans were producing more than enough half-hour comedy shows for both countries. In any case, Canadians were above turning out *schlock*. Our limited resources were going to be devoted to quality programming. If some people preferred American crap to all the good things the CBC could give them, that was their loss.

It wasn't until the mid-1960s that the CBC decided it had an obligation to try to produce drama that was not only good but popular as well. The result was series like *Wojeck* and *Quentin Durgens*. But despite these successes, the CBC stayed clear of half-hour comedies. We'd come to believe so firmly that we couldn't or shouldn't compete that we didn't even try. Canadians with a talent for such programming — the Winnipeg writer Perry Rosemond, for instance — simply packed up and moved to the U.S. It wasn't until *Delilah* in 1973 that the CBC tried again to produce a comedy series.

Delilah was a disaster. That's not surprising if one considers that at the three major U.S. networks, with their huge programme development budgets, only one in seven pilots gets on the air. The CBC's *Delilah* was a programme without adequate planning or funding and was being attempted at a network that had had no experience with half-hour comedy series for more than a decade. The unbelievably bad scripts were based on the assumption that the idea of a woman barber in an Ontario small town is inherently funny. The programme was laughed off the air. The experience taught the CBC a valuable lesson — that producing a successful half-hour comedy series wasn't nearly as easy as it looked. What was required was the TV equivalent of a good rep company turning out an original thirty-minute play every week. The central idea and main characters had to be strong enough to sustain the show.

When John Hirsch took over the CBC's drama department in the mid-1970s, he brought Perry Rosemond back from the U.S. to develop a comedy series. His pilot was awful, but the programme, *King of Kensington*, was given the go-ahead anyway. Those involved would have to learn on the job. It was a daring decision. *King of Kensington*, a domestic comedy based on the life of Larry King (Al Waxman), who ran a variety store and lived in an ethnically mixed area of downtown Toronto, came on air in September 1975. Initial reaction to the programme was largely unfavourable. Most reviewers agreed with Douglas Marshall, who wrote in *TV Guide* that "a network that can screen *Rhoda* and *All in the Family* on Mondays, *M*A*S*H* and *Mary Tyler Moore* on Fridays, and expect us to admire *King* on Thursdays should have its collective head examined." Things were so bad during the early weeks of the show that Rosemond urged those involved in it to stay away from the CBC's head offices to avoid being demoralized by what they heard. (The show was taped in studios a few blocks away.) At the end of its first thirteen episodes, *King of Kensington* came close to being cancelled.

There was a lot that was wrong. The programme lacked the production values of American shows. Its colour wasn't as crisp, its editing wasn't as sharp. Its scripts were terribly uneven. But there were even more things that were right. Waxman himself turned in a fine performance every week, even when scripts were at their worst. As Frank Penn of the Ottawa *Citizen* put it, "There's something about the man. Under the easy grin and the...well-nourished cheeks, there's a sense of [the kind of] inner energy that illuminated John Vernon's Wojeck and [Gordon Pinsent's] Quentin Durgens...." Fiona Reid as his wife seemed to grow in her role from show to show. (*King of Kensington* was never quite the same after she left the show to pursue her stage career.) There were fine guest appearances by Peter Kastner among others. With the exceptions of Gladys King (Helene Winston) as the stereotypical Jewish mother and Max (John Dee) as the stereotypical befuddled old person on TV, the characters on *King of Kensington* were less predictable than those on American shows.

Mostly what I liked was the show's pace, its mood, its tone. Compared to the people on *King of Kensington*, those on American shows such as *All in the Family* seemed speeded up. *King of Kensington* felt like a 1950s American comedy rather than one from the 1970s. Even in its most cynical moments, its view of human nature was less bleak. In an early show, for instance, Larry, who's a bit of a knee-jerk liberal, can't sleep. "Cathy," he sighs, "the prison system isn't working." "I know," she replies sympathetically. "But the fridge isn't working, the shower isn't working, and seven per cent of the public isn't working. Let's go to bed!" On *King of Kensington* the line was warm, human. Imagine Archie Bunker delivering the same line.

The mood of most American 1970s situation comedies was pessimistic and misanthropic. Bob (Hartley) Newhart, as David Feldman noted in the *Journal of Popular Culture*, was a psychologist who couldn't communicate. The city he inhabited (Chicago) was a concrete jungle. It had none of the warm, friendly city streets Jim Anderson used to drive along in *Father Knows Best*. Hartley's practice was thriving, yet all of his patients were hopeless cases. We never once saw him help anyone. Norman Lear's *All in the Family* was a kind of ethnic joke turned into a series. The characters in this show, like those in *Maude, Phyllis* and *Alice*, were so loud, so hard-edged, so inhuman that, for the most part, I found them repulsive. As Arthur Berger puts it in *The TV-Guided American*, such programmes offer the reverse of the myth of the 1950s domestic comedy — "the myth of the American as 'Nature's Nobleman', as a clean-cut, hard-working, rugged, self-reliant individual who achieves his goals through force of willpower and determination. Instead what we find are a collection of weak-willed, middle-class...neurotic losers who find themselves in awkward situations all the time."*

People on *King of Kensington* had softer edges than those on many American comedies; they were never afraid to show real feelings. Indeed, at times they were as blatantly sentimental as the characters in a film by Frank Capra and, as in Capra, laughter and tears were never far apart. In one episode, for instance, Larry and Cathy have been trying for some time to have a baby. Cathy is on fertility drugs, and there's a possibility she's finally become pregnant. Gladys rushes out to buy a pink snowsuit. Larry comes home with some tiny boxing gloves. While the two of them tease one another about their purchases, Cathy returns from the doctor to inform them she's not preg-

---

* Compare the mood and tone of these American shows with that of *Hangin' In*, a current CBC sitcom in which, in their own bumbling ways, Kate (Lally Cadeau) and her colleagues at a downtown drop-in centre actually help troubled teenagers.

nant. In a moving scene, she insists it's time Larry was tested to find out if *he's* to blame: "I've been through fertility drugs, hormones...God knows what I've done to my body," she screams. "I'm not going through another thing till I find out if it's you." It turns out that it *is* Larry. On his return from the doctor, and just before he tells Cathy, Larry picks up the pink snowsuit lying on the couch and hugs it. It's a lovely moment. Within ten minutes the same pink snowsuit has evoked laughter and tears.

That's an example of a *King of Kensington* script at its best. But the same show also contained examples of *Kensington* at its worst. (It's the mixture of good and bad that made so many episodes frustrating.) A couple of pregnant women, appearing grotesque, sit in a doctor's office looking at male nudes in *Viva* and *Playgirl* and saying, "What's so big about that?" and "I didn't know he was Jewish." What happened was that the writers and producers got cold feet and resorted to smart-ass humour.

Part of the problem was that *King of Kensington* had few experienced staff — especially writers and editors. One needed only compare the credits on *King* with those on even atrocious American sitcoms such as *Alice*. The original story for each episode of *Alice* is written by two people, the teleplay by a third. There are two story consultants, two story editors and two executive story editors. Nine people for each script, and all separate from the production staff. Most of the early scripts for *King of Kensington* were written by Louis del Grande and Jack Humphrey, who also produced each episode.

IV

Of course the CBC sometimes does high jpm programmes. But they tend to be fast-paced shows with a difference.

Consider *Seeing Things*, the CBC's excellent mystery/ comedy series about a Toronto newspaper reporter who has ESP. Louie Ciccone as played by Louis del Grande looks Canadian: he's fortyish, bald, overweight and a klutz. And like the ordinary guy in a Hitchcock movie who has stumbled across a crime about which he knows too much, Louie can't rest until he's sorted things out. (There's nothing quite like *Seeing Things* on American television at the present time. But there have been somewhat similar programmes in the past — *McMillan and Wife*, *Columbo* and *The Rockford Files*, for example.)

The plots on *Seeing Things* always revolve around murder, but the writers' guide for the show seems almost embarrassed by the fact. There's something wonderfully Canadian about the following lines: "We seem to be stuck with murder. It's probably possible to centre a story around some other crime, but it sure would not be easy. Murder, the threat of murder, and mysterious disappearances seem to be the stuff of the genre. Even theft, which seems the next most logical crime, usually requires that murder be connected with it somewhere in the course of the story. A few words about murder. We are not of the multi-body school of writers. There are four killings in our first three shows (five, actually, but the fifth is just talked about, never seen). We prefer the story to turn on a single killing; less, hopefully, being more. If you feel that more than one person must die, be prepared to justify it. Murder, unfortunately, usually involves violence. But we want the violence to be minimal. Try to be creative when you have to show violent acts; you can shock the viewer with the suddenness or the unexpected quality of an event without dwelling on gore or mayhem...."

Despite its good, detailed writers' guide, the scripts for *Seeing Things* themselves sometimes leave something to be desired. Their strength lies in their delightful portrayal of Louie as a bumbler, whose only tools, as one reviewer put it, are "his outdated moral sense and...visions, and whose muscle is only in his fast-talking mouth." Their strength also lies in their witty dialogue. ("Just because we slept together doesn't mean we aren't separated anymore.") And their off-beat characters — an elderly woman, for instance, who sells Louie her piano so she can buy state-of-the-art video equipment. Their weakness is plots that frequently feel contrived.

V

And then there's family drama, a form which, with the demise of *Little House on the Prairie*, is almost non-existent on American television. *The Beachcombers* is the longest-lived and most popular of the CBC's family dramas but it's too cartoonish for my liking. Still, compared to American television, it's a non-violent show on which, as producer Don Williams says, "No one ever gets shot, stabbed or beaten and on which fisticuffs are used only for comedic purposes." And like *Seeing Things*, *The Beachcombers* is old-fashioned in its concern with family — albeit in this case the extended family of Nick Adonidas (Bruno Gerussi), an overgrown kid who's passionately in love with life.

Danger Bay is also concerned with family and positive role models. The show is about the adventures of Grant "Doc" Roberts (Donnelly Rhodes), a veterinarian and crusading Curator of Marine Mammals at the Vancouver Aquarium. Roberts is a single parent with a fourteen-year-old son and a twelve-year-old daughter. Joyce Carter (Deborah Wakeham) is an independent-minded seaplane pilot who frequently flies Roberts on difficult rescue missions. Like *The Beachcomers*, *Danger Bay* isn't one of my favourite shows. But it is distinctly Canadian. Some years ago American television critic Neil Compton taught at George Williams in Montreal. He watched a lot of Canadian television and compared it to American TV this way: "All television systems offer a high proportion of poor programs; but the earnest, muddling, amateurish trash of Canada seems to me bad in a more endearing way than the mindless, slick, mechanical trash that clutters American airwaves." Right on. I'll take the earnestness of *The Beachcomers* and *Danger Bay* over the mindlessness of *Dukes of Hazzard* and *The A-Team*.

Danger Bay is a co-production involving the CBC, Disney Films and Telefilm Canada. Telefilm Canada, which came into existence in July 1983, and which replaced the Canadian Film Development Corporation (CFDC), is a federal agency which helps finance Canadian-made films and television programmes. Its Canadian Broadcast Programme Development Fund now invests up to forty-nine per cent of the production costs of TV programmes; the remainder comes from broadcasters and private sources. In order to qualify, programmes must originate with private producers, have substantial Canadian content, and be aired in prime time on a Canadian network or station.

Telefilm money has played a particularly important part in the recent increase in family dramas on the CBC. Other Broadcast Fund projects include the ninety-minute drama *Hockey Night* and the *Sons and Daughters* series. *Hockey Night* is a well-made and touching film about the difficulties a teenage girl in a small Ontario town has trying to play goal on the boys' team. A good script and fine acting, especially by Megan Follows as the girl and Rick Moranis as the coach, prevent the film from being mawkish. Sexual stereotyping is one of the problems of growing up dealt with in *Sons and Daughters*, a thirteen-part series of half-hour programmes based on Canadian short stories. In

Boys and Girls Megan Follows is a young farm girl in the 1940s who rebels against the traditional female role her parents impose on her. *Boys and Girls* is based on an Alice Munro short story. When the programme won an Academy Award for Best Short Film, Megan Follows commented, "The film was different and refreshing, especially for an American audience. They don't get those nice, simple stories there — a story that doesn't have to prove anything — a story that just 'is'." Other stories in the series include *Cornet at Night*, based on a Sinclair Ross story, and *Olden Days Coat*, adapted from a story by Margaret Laurence.

VI

Charlie Grant's War is an example of the kind of "serious" drama that the CBC, at its best, can produce, drama unlike almost anything available on American commercial television. The only exceptions in recent years that I can think of are *Playing for Time* with Vanessa Redgrave and *Death of a Salesman* with Dustin Hoffman. Mostly what passes for serious drama on American TV are mini-series, such as *Shogun* and *Rich Man, Poor Man*, that are long on jpm's and short on thoughtfulness and character development. *Roots* was an exception. *Holocaust* was a kind of exception. As Clive James argued, "It can't be done and perhaps ought never to have been attempted, but if you leave those questions aside then there should be room to admit the possibility that *Holocaust* wasn't really all that bad. At its best it gave a modicum of dramatic life to some notoriously intractable moral issues, and even at its worst was no disgrace."

Charlie Grant's War, a two-and-a-half-hour made-for-TV movie written by Anna Sandor, produced by Bill

Gough and starring R.H. Thomson, concerns the gradual politicization of a Canadian *bon vivant* living in Austria in the years before the Second World War. When Charlie Grant's Jewish friends are affected by the growing anti-semitism, he tries to help them leave. He then realizes that he feels compelled to help other Jews too and persuades a reluctant Austrian bureaucrat to arrange fake exit visas. "This may be the only chance we get in our lives to do something extraordinary," Charlie says. The irony, as Irving Abella and Harold Troper's recent book *None Is Too Many* makes clear, is that Charlie Grant's own country isn't accepting Jewish immigrants; it seems they don't assimilate well enough.

R.H. Thomson's performance is superb. Critic Martin Knelman wrote, Thomson "has managed to make Grant into a character rather than a mouthpiece for noble ideals....Thomson never makes the mistake of overplaying. He tones down scenes that could have been phony, and he keeps building small human details and levels of ambiguity within the character. This subtle, complex performance is what draws the viewer in...." Grant first puts some of his own money on the line. Next he puts his business on the line. Then his freedom. And finally his life.

Not all of the CBC's serious drama is so sombre. Consider *Chautauqua Girl*. In the years before film and radio created mass entertainment, a kind of travelling cultural circus called Chautauqua opened up new worlds of music and drama and ideas to people who didn't know such things existed. For a generation of Canadians, especially in remote communities in the West, the Chautauqua tent was of incalculable importance. It was to its time what saddlebag preachers (or circuit riders) had been a century earlier. Both the saddlebag preachers and the Chautauqua were products of Methodism and its obsession with education, with opening windows.

Chautauqua Girl is a made-for-CBC television movie about one of the independent young advance women who prepared each town — Fairville, Alberta, in this case — for the show's arrival. Written and produced by Jeannine Locke, *Chautauqua Girl* stars Janet-Laine Green as Sally Driscoll and Terence Kelly as would-be politician Neil McCallum, a tough, lonely farmer. It's the summer of 1921, the summer in which the United Farmers of Alberta won a landslide victory over the Liberals, and *Chautauqua Girl* has something of the glow of a magic realist painting as it captures that time.

In just over a decade, the Chautauqua tent in Canada had been replaced by public broadcasting, a new kind of Chautauqua. CBC radio producer Andrew Allan tells of being recognized by a young woman on a train in the late 1940s. Her life had literally been transformed by listening to his *Stage* series of hour-long radio dramas. "We live on a farm, away up north of Edmonton," she told Allan. "We're just plain people, I guess. We haven't got any books to speak of, or pictures, or music, or anything. But I have a little radio in my room. Every Sunday night I go up there to listen to your plays. All week I wait for that time. It's wonderful. It's a whole new world for me. I began to read books because of your plays — all kinds of books I never thought I'd be interested in. And now I'm on my way to Vancouver to stay with my aunt and in the fall I'm starting at the university. And it's all because of you and your plays." I suspect there are countless others who could say similar things about the effect CBC programmes have had on them.

The Canadian Competition

I

Obviously, there are exceptions to the patterns I've described on both sides of the border. *Mister Rogers' Neighbourhood*, as I've already mentioned, is an example of a good, slow-paced children's programme on American television. The gentle, low-key *Mister Rogers* is reminiscent of *Mr. Dressup* in its mood and tone. It's not surprising to discover that Ernie Coombes (Mr. Dressup) and Fred Rogers (Mr. Rogers) are former colleagues. Like *Sesame Street*, *Mister Rogers* is a PBS production, but whereas *Sesame Street* models itself on commercial television and would fit just as well there, *Mister Rogers* is the kind of programme only public television can provide. The only similar show on commercial television in recent years, the charming *Captain Kangaroo*, was a mainstay of early morning TV until CBS realized there was far more money to be made by providing yet more programming for infomaniacs. *Captain Kangaroo* was relegated to weekends at 6 a.m. and is now off the air entirely. Its star now hosts an animated series of adaptations from children's literature on Saturday mornings.

There *have* been good, slow-paced adult programmes on U.S. television — some extremely well-written, half-hour sitcoms, for example, that have dealt sensitively with some of the larger social and moral concerns of the past decade and a half. The war in Vietnam provided an appropriate backdrop for *M*A*S*H*, an anti-war comedy set in a hospital during the Korean War. *Mary Tyler Moore*, which took place at a TV station in middle America, dealt with the problems of being a single career woman in a world that was rapidly changing. *Barney Miller* told us week after week — as a procession of criminals, victims and crazies passed through the dreary Greenwich Village police station — that the only way to respond to the screwed up world we live in is with compassion and good humour. And there have been some good, well-written, slow-paced hour-long dramatic series as well. *Paper Chase* concerned a first-year law student, James T. Hart, taking a course in contract law from a famous but irascible professor (John Houseman) who drove his students relentlessly. Elizabeth Logan was a fellow student with strong feminist views. *Lou Grant* was centred on the hard-nosed city editor of the Los Angeles *Tribune* and the people and issues he dealt with. None of these programmes is still on the air. Grant Tinker, President of NBC, says that *Mary Tyler Moore* (which he produced) couldn't make it on TV today. It embarrasses him that his own network's top show is *The A-Team*.

Not every high jpm programme currently on American television is mindless. Both *Hill Street Blues* and *Cagney and Lacey* deal with the professional and personal lives of police men and women (for example, several episodes of *Cagney and Lacey* dealt with Mary Beth Lacey's breast cancer and treatment) and both are examples of hour-long episodic shows that are fast-paced yet realistic and thoughtful, as much concerned with character development as they are with plot. A year ago, I would have included *St. Elsewhere* on this list but in recent months that show has become strangely surreal in its plot twists. For example, one patient died from being squeezed to death by an adjustable bed.

And occasionally one finds good and/or thought-provoking drama on American commercial TV. *The Burning Bed*, a harrowing play starring Farrah Fawcett, was concerned with wife-beating. *Silence of the Heart* with Mariette Hartley was about the guilt and agony of teenage suicide.

II

There are exceptions on the Canadian side of the border too. CTV, for example. As the Association of Canadian Television and Radio Artists (ACTRA) put it during CTV's 1978 licence renewal hearings, "Since its formation in 1961, the CTV television network has acted as an effective and powerful catalyst in the Americanization of Canadian mass culture. Not only do... programmes produced in the United States make up almost ninety per cent of the peak 8 p.m. to 10 p.m. viewing hours...but the quality of these programmes is of such a nature that CTV was called by the LaMarsh Commission on Media Violence the most violent network on the continent."

The Canadian Radio and Television Commission (CRTC) was created in 1968 to administer and uphold the Broadcasting Act. According to the act, the Canadian broadcasting system, which is made up of public and private components, "should...safeguard, enrich and strengthen the cultural, political, social and economic fabric of Canada." That's no mean task, and the CRTC has the responsibility to see that it happens. In its wisdom, the CRTC concluded more than a decade ago that CTV wasn't doing enough Canadian drama. So when the commission renewed CTV's licence in 1973, it urged the network to "develop more drama programming with Canadian themes, concerns and locales." Very little was done. When the CRTC next renewed CTV's licence in 1976, it reiterated its request, this time more firmly. "The

Commission expects the network, in future schedules, to correct the deficiency of no weekly Canadian drama...." Again, nothing happened.

The sad fact is that when it comes to enforcing its rules, the CRTC has been and continues to be a paper tiger. Until very recently, no radio or television station has ever had a licence revoked. The worst that has happened has been the CRTC's attaching conditions to a licence — renewing it but saying, "We're renewing this licence on condition that you do such and such." In 1979, partly in response to interventions from ACTRA and other groups, the CRTC attached conditions to CTV's licence. It is a condition of CTV's licence, said the commission, "that twenty-six hours of original new Canadian drama be presented during the 1981-82 season."

CTV's president, Murray Chercover, was incensed. He took the CRTC to court, arguing that the commission's regulations don't define what a "Canadian" theme is. The same Murray Chercover had told the CRTC's 1975 licence renewal hearings, "We need no condition on our licence to encourage us to become a major producer of Canadian programmes....We have an obligation...to provide a schedule in the national interest."

The truth is that there's a fundamental contradiction between the high-minded objectives of the Broadcasting Act and the financial interest of private broadcasters. It's in the financial interest of CTV that as many American, and American-looking, programmes as possible be screened. That's where the big advertising dollars are to be made. And large numbers of viewers, after all, do prefer American — high jpm — programmes. Advertisers, it must be noted, don't buy individual programmes; they buy blocks of viewers. The more viewers, the more money they pay. Making money is what private broadcasting is about. For instance, CTV produced only one Canadian drama series in the period we're talking about — a rather good half-hour situation comedy, *Excuse My French*. It cost $780,000 to produce and brought in $574,300 in advertising revenue, for a net loss of $205,700. *Excuse My French* had no international sales and was cancelled after its second season. Compare that with the cost of buying an entire season of the hour-long *Kojak* (1974-75) for $212,000 and the $1.76 million in ad revenue it brought in. CTV has no financial incentive to make Canadian programmes.

Cultural politics, however, demands that CTV and other private broadcasters talk as if they believe in the aims of the CRTC and the Broadcasting Act. Here again, for example, is Murray Chercover (1971): "The sense of Canadian identity will not be served by cheap, mindless game shows." No one, not even Mel Hurtig, speaking on behalf of the Committee for an Independent Canada, could have put it better. But while Chercover continues to say one thing, CTV's programming says quite another. In a study for the United Nations done by the U.S.-based National Coalition on Television Violence, CTV was described as the most violent of thirty networks around the world. (The Ontario government's LaMarsh Commission on violence in the media had only thought it the most violent network on the continent.) Prime time on CTV, said the U.N. report, is a "ghetto of American violence." CTV's programming is for the most part indistinguishable from the slick, high jpm content of American television. Maggie Siggins writes in a biography of John Bassett, former owner of CFTO in Toronto, "If CFTO, the flagship of CTV, was to land mysteriously in the night in Toledo, Ohio, few viewers would find the programming strange, so essentially American is the station in style and scheduling."

CTV's sole contribution to Canadian drama in recent

years has been *The Littlest Hobo*, an atrocious reincarnation of a popular American TV show of the 1960s. The show features a German shepherd named Hobo, a kind of canine Lone Ranger or Jack Kerouac, who ceaselessly wanders from place to place through an anonymous landscape. (CTV, it seems, wouldn't want anyone to suspect this series takes place in Canada. That might affect American sales.) Hobo is clearly the most intelligent being on the show and he specializes in rescuing incredibly dumb humans (usually guest Americans) from one catastrophe after another. In one episode a bush plane crashes a hundred miles from nowhere. Who should happen to be strolling through the dense bush four feet away from the crash but our hero? Everyone on board the plane is a stereotype. There's a school principal named Proust, for example, who's a supercilious twit. (Writers of awful programmes such as this frequently include a literary allusion as a way of reassuring their friends that they haven't really sold out.) No one on the plane has the foggiest idea what to do. Hobo patiently prods each one into action. *The Littlest Hobo* is an example of a cheap, mindless programme that's relatively low in jpm's.

Then there are CTV's half-hour contributions to Canadian variety programming. *Circus* is a high jpm collection of circus and vaudeville routines that, like *The Littlest Hobo*, disguises the fact that it's Canadian. The acts on *Circus* aren't all that great, but what the show lacks in quality, it makes up for in loudness. Indeed, if there were an award for the loudest show on Canadian TV, *Circus* would win. The announcer doesn't just tell us what's going to happen next, he shouts it. The audience's applause, which has been considerably sweetened and amplified, is deafening, as is the musical background. *Bizarre*, hosted by American comedian John Bynor, consists of three or four adolescent skits, usually about sex. Many of the jolts on this show are achieved by beeping and blipping out things that are too "dirty" for us to hear or see: a three-beep sketch about Cinderella losing her glass brassiere; an eight-beep, two-blip sketch about dirty animal tricks. (The freedom to deal with sex on television has meant, for the most part, treating it as a dirty joke.) *Snow Job*, which is just as sleazy as *Bizarre*, is the only *Canadian* show of the bunch. It's set in a ski resort near Montreal, and the humour consists of jokes about sex and jokes that treat French-Canadians as imbeciles. *Thrill of a Lifetime* patronizes those who want a dream fulfilled, usually by meeting an American celebrity. Shannon Tweed of Newfoundland became a celebrity after appearing on the show and meeting the people at *Playboy*. A man gets to sing and play guitar with Johnny Cash.

One other variety programme is now gone. *Grand Old Country*'s host, Ronnie Prophet, I understand, has graduated to the U.S. Certainly he made it clear that he thought it was a mistake for Canadian country singers to sound Canadian. "I think there is a certain sound that you have to acquire to become accepted in the U.S. You can listen to a Canadian song and even though the music [is] the same as a Nashville song, the singer says his words differently. When you play it on an American station, the listeners aren't used to it. It sounds foreign." It was important for Canadian country singers to sound American. *Grand Old Country*, Prophet proudly believed, was "more Americanized than any Canadian [country] show" had ever been. I'm sure he was right. Alan Thicke of *The Alan Thicke Show* has also now graduated to the U.S. His talk show was replaced by *Don Harron* (which in turn has been replaced by a show hosted by Peter Feniak). As with his predecessor's, most of Harron's guests were American. A typical show features Stephen Wright, a young American comedian. He's funny, but we've heard all his jokes before on *The Tonight Show*. Lorne Greene, another Canadian graduate, comes on full of compliments for the genius of Don Harron. Greene is there to promote *The New Wilderness*, a show he's hosting for CTV. (*The New Wilderness* makes use of excellent footage — of ostriches, for example — but, as usual, there's nothing in the content of the show to suggest it was made in Canada.)

Then there's *Live It Up*. According to a CTV press release, "Today's great life-question seems to be: 'What's in it for me?' *Live It Up* answers this question." It does so by telling us how many sheets there are in a roll of toilet paper (336). "An audience needs jolts," says *Live It Up*'s executive producer Jack McGaw. "They like to be jolted in one way or another, either surprised with information or with pacings or humour. *Live It Up*'s audience gets lots of jolts."

CTV's contributions to Canadian children's programming are embarrassingly bad. Uncle Bobby is smarmy, and the host of *Romper Room*, Miss Fran, is patronizing. She mostly ignores the real children in her presence and talks to those in TV land. The kids in the studio are dull, and the show seems designed to keep them that way. No one is ever allowed to say no or to go off on a tangent. "You know, children," says Miss Fran to some kid who hasn't listened to one of her boring comments, "when grown-ups speak, they usually have something to say, and we should try to be good listeners." The kids on *Romper Room* all wear their Sunday best — no one is allowed to get dirty. One has a sense that Miss Fran is a closet authoritarian afraid that anarchy will be let loose if she gives an inch. I would certainly never deliberately expose a child of mine to *Romper Room*.

In 1982, after three years, the CRTC won its battle with CTV over whether the commission had the right to request the network to be more Canadian. The case went all the way to the Supreme Court. But in a very real sense the CRTC won nothing. CTV's heart just isn't in it when it comes to producing distinctly Canadian shows. And in fairness to CTV, there's no money in doing so. No amount of prodding or attaching of conditions will change that. And the CRTC doesn't believe in taking licences away once they've been awarded.

There are some exceptions in CTV's schedule, but they are all in the area of news,* current affairs and sports. Every morning *Canada AM* offers an in-depth look at the day's headlines as Norm Perry and Linda MacLennan interview prominent newsmakers and their critics. The programme is not unlike CBC radio's *As It Happens* or *The Journal* on television. *W5* is CTV's answer to *the fifth estate*. Although it tends to tell us what we already know if we read the papers regularly, it occasionally also does original reporting. A first-rate item, for example, focused on the cause of a 1978 Air Canada crash at Toronto's Malton Airport that killed two and injured forty-seven others. New information gathered by *W5* had suggested the pilot was *not* at fault. (Air Canada had blamed and reassigned him.)

Still, it seems to me, *W5* has never wholly regained its credibility from a sloppily researched item of several years ago ("Campus Giveaway") that, among other errors, misidentified Chinese Canadians in University of Toronto classrooms as "foreigners." "Campus Giveaway" suggested there were too many non-Canadians attending our universities and colleges. CTV and *W5* executives fool-

---

* Ontario's CTV affiliates chose not to cover the recent provincial election on a regular basis. Donald Willcox of CKCO in Kitchener said that his station would assign reporters to the three political leaders only "when they're in our coverage area....But we're not going to travel all over the province." Willcox cited "economic considerations" and went on to say, "In my own mind, I wonder whether the average viewer takes a real interest in provincial politics."

ishly stonewalled for seven months before offering an abject apology. Another error cost CTV not just more credibility but $1,372,048 in damages — the largest libel award in Canadian history. *W5* falsely accused a company of improperly disposing of industrial waste.

There are two CTV programmes I haven't mentioned — *Question Period* and *Definition*. Both are special. They look and feel like CBC programmes that have somehow wandered onto the wrong network. If what characterizes most of CTV's programming is mindlessness, what characterizes these shows is quality of mind. On *Question Period*, which is buried in the Sunday afternoon schedule, four journalists interview a prominent newsmaker for half an hour. The programme used to be hosted by Bruce Phillips, CTV's most able political journalist. But Phillips has gone into public relations and been replaced by Pamela Wallin. *Definition* is a sophisticated word game that tests one's wit. Two teams of two compete with one another to identify puns. (A graffiti artist is a "wall nut.") The host of *Definition* is Jim Perry, who also hosts *Sale of the Century*, a high jpm American game show. The contrast between *Definition* and *Sale of the Century* is a wonder to behold.

III

CTV, of course, isn't the only offender. Only the most obvious. Global TV's record leaves much to be desired too. But unlike CTV, Global actually made an effort to put money into Canadian production when it first came on the air in 1974. Global's first president, Al Bruner, had promised the CRTC he would invest at least $8 million in Canada's production industry during Global's first year. He kept his promise, but it almost forced his company into bankruptcy.

The largest amount of money, about $1.7 million, went

into *Everything Goes*, a ninety-minute, five-times-weekly variety programme, which viewers would have been hard-pressed to identify as Canadian. The success of the show, after all, depended on American sales (which didn't come). The host of *Everything Goes*, comedian Norm Crosby, was American; most of his guests were American; many of the Canadians who appeared on *Everything Goes* — Monty Hall, for instance — were there because they'd made it in America. Despite all this, much of the best material in the show frequently was Canadian — Moe Koffman's band, Dave Broadfoot's Corporal Renfrew, Earl Pomerantz's *schlemiel*.

This Programme Is About Sex, another show of this early period, was based on a good and simple idea — a group of men and women sitting around a table talking about what it meant to be a man or woman, single, married or whatever. But there were serious problems with the show. Not only was its title misleading, but its host, Sol Gordon, an American professor of family studies, actually seemed uncomfortable when the programme did deal with sex. (Again we had an American host to help promote U.S. sales.) One woman finally asked him, "Why do you have that lewd look on your face when you talk about affairs?" Occasionally, mostly when Sol Gordon wasn't talking, the conversation was extremely good — only to be interrupted by a commercial. There are few things more irritating than having good conversation (or film, or drama) interrupted and trivialized this way. That's probably why most talk shows are hosted by the likes of Merv Griffin; that way only rarely is anything worth listening to interrupted.

Pierre Berton brought two new Canadian programmes to Global — *My Country* and *The Great Debate*. On *My Country*, Berton told the story of the exploits of some important or interesting Canadian, making use of photographs, maps, artifacts — whatever he could lay his hands on — to bring the story to life. *The Great Debate* brought together major figures to debate issues of national and international importance. The programme continues to be produced by the independent Hamilton station CHCH.

The other Canadian shows that began at this time were *Witness to Yesterday* and *World of Wicks*. *Witness to Yesterday*, which was always interesting, brought history to life with dramatized interviews between Patrick Watson and actors playing historical figures. The programme continues in re-run. *World of Wicks* was made up of delightfully offbeat interviews by cartoonist Ben Wicks. My favourite Wicks interview was with David Niven, who told the story — true, apparently — of how he got a frostbitten penis while skiing and had to stand in the john of a pub dunking the afflicted organ in brandy to thaw it out. When someone came in and wondered what Niven was doing, he replied that he always pissed in a brandy glass.

And Global offered a fresh approach to sports reporting. Global's camera work during World Hockey Association games didn't compare with that of *Hockey Night in Canada*. But that was more than made up for by the honest colour commentary of Peter Gzowski and Ken Dryden, who actually *criticized* what was going on on the ice. This player never backchecked, that one was foolish enough to keep shooting from outside the blue line. When Gzowski asked Dryden a question, it sounded as if he really wanted to know the answer, as if he would have asked the same question even if they hadn't been on the air.

Potentially, Global's most important contribution lay in the area of Canadian film. The network bought television rights to thirty films from Quebec — films by Gilles Carle, Jean-Pierre Lefevbre, and others whose work was virtually unknown in English Canada. Global agreed to have the films dubbed into English to theatrical standards — a move that not only stimulated Montreal's dubbing industry but that meant the films would subsequently be available for distribution in the English-speaking international market. Unfortunately, the films were so badly dubbed that they gave Québécois film and filmmakers a bad name among those unlucky enough to watch them.*

These things — and more — were done during Global's first year. As a result, the network almost went bankrupt. In the years that followed, Global did as little Canadian programming as possible — as little as CTV — as it refinanced and reorganized itself. The one notable exception was Global's decision in the mid-1970s to schedule the brilliant satirical show *SCTV* for half an hour a week. In 1985, however, Global has shown signs of again becoming more active in Canadian programming. It's co-produced with the National Film Board, Atlantis Films and Telefilm Canada eight half-hour adaptations of Canadian short stories for *Global Playhouse*. Global has produced (also with the assistance of Telefilm Canada) a two-hour TV version of Stratford's *The Country Wife*. Other projects are in the works.

Independent Canadian stations such as Toronto's CITY-TV also succeed by looking as American as possible. CITY's hour-long *CityPulse* newscasts are the fastest-paced of any I've seen on Canadian television. The station's newscasters are all personalities and the news is clearly showbiz. Even the couturier who provides host Gord Martineau's wardrobe gets a credit. But it's not just Martineau — everyone on this show is beautifully (or outrageously) dressed. The mike is treated as a hot potato as it's passed from one reporter to another, each of whom

---

* Some of these films are now appearing on Pay-TV. I recently saw Gilles Carle's *Les Mâles* on Superchannel. I turned it off quickly.

tells us what he or she is going to tell us when his or her turn comes next. Later in the show the process is repeated and each tells us yet again what he or she has told us. The whole thing leaves one rather breathless. And the local news footage on CITY not only is more rapidly edited but is far more graphic than any I've seen in Canada.*

CITY is also responsible for *20 Minute Workout*, the most widely syndicated Canadian programme ever. The show, now seen on more than 100 stations in Canada and the U.S., features three young women dressed in skimpy bodysuits doing aerobic exercises on a revolving stage to a background of pulsating music. The women affect the look of sex kittens; one of them encourages us in an icky little girl voice to "come on" and to move "faster, faster." Meanwhile we intercut between and among cameras that caress the three bodies from all angles. The cameras focus in particular on the women's buttocks and crotches, and at times it's difficult to follow what's going on because of the strange camera angles. (Sometimes the women seem to have more than two legs.) What *20 Minute Workout* offers us is high jpm, soft-core porn. Canadian high jpm, soft-core porn.

And CITY also produces *MuchMusic*, a twenty-four hour Pay-TV rock video show — the ultimate in high jpm television. The movement, the edits, the noise never stop. Neither does my incomprehension at what's going on most of the time.

---

* That wasn't always the case. Before the CBC moved *The National*'s time slot, CITY-TV's 10 p.m. newscast offered by far the most thoughtful local news in Toronto. And it was comparatively slow-paced. Every night the always gracious host Bill Cameron (now with *The Journal* and *Midday*) did a phone-in segment, usually on a serious subject, and ended the show with a brief editorial comment, which was always either interesting or amusing or both. Bill Cameron himself now refers to the new *CityPulse* as "disco news."

IV

None of this is to say the CBC doesn't occasionally fall into the same trap in its eagerness to make its programmes look American. Take *The René Simard Show*. When I told a public relations man at the CBC in the late 1970s that two of my children liked Simard, he started rushing around his office handing me things — a big blue Simard poster, a couple of Simard records. "Unfortunately," he said as he gave me the records, "they're partly in French."

"Unfortunately, they're partly in French." What a wonderful line. So — comment dirais-je? — English-Canadian. Here was this likable, good-looking, not untalented, Québécois kid who came on our English-Canadian television screens saying things like, "Good evening, ladies and gentlemen, or, as we say in French, 'Hi'." Had Simard been working out of a studio in Quebec, that line just might have worked. But *The René Simard Show* was coming to us from British Columbia. It was a *regional* offering. And in case anyone wondered about that, CBC executive Jack McAndrew announced: "The fact that René Simard is French has nothing to do with the show." An authentic regional programme, *Don Messer's Jubilee*, had been cancelled a few years earlier because CBC executives in central Canada found Messer embarrassingly provincial. Now we were to have an inauthentic, executive-approved regional programme. (The only regular CBC regional programming now consists of *The Beachcombers* and *Danger Bay* from British Columbia and *Hymn Sing* from Winnipeg.)

It quickly became obvious as one watched *The René Simard Show* that it looked and felt American. For one thing, Simard's guests were almost all from the U.S. — big-name stars like Diahann Carroll, Sandy Duncan and Andy Williams — none of whom seemed able to pronounce Simard's name. The material Simard performed was American. And the style was American. Simard almost never stood still. Neither did the camera. From the control room we got double and triple superimpositions and in the background there were flashing and reflecting lights. The words "René" and "disco" kept going on and off in neon. It was hard on the eyes.

One of the results of all the technical hocus-pocus was that we were distracted from noticing that Simard was having trouble with his voice. He could still belt out certain kinds of songs, such as Jacques Brel's "If we only have love." But his voice was changing, and he didn't have either the range or the control for most ballads. What with choruses, duets, over-dubs and the like, we didn't hear that much of Simard himself. Perhaps that was just as well.

It wasn't just Simard's voice that was changing. So was his style. He was working hard at a new "adult" image and having trouble bringing it off. He'd switched over-night from being a frisky, ingenuous adolescent in jump-suits to being a young man on the make in snug-around-the-crotch leisure suits, who stood (surrounded by gorgeous women) with his legs spread in what was supposed to be a sexy pose. Too often, however, it seemed as if he were standing that way simply because his pants were too tight. He was no longer singing songs like "Ave Maria" designed to gladden the hearts of mothers who wished their sons were like him. Now they got "Mrs. Robinson."

René Simard's overwhelming ambition, or at least the ambition of his manager, Guy Cloutier, was that Simard would graduate and make it big in the U.S. — perhaps as NBC's or CBS's answer to *Donny and Marie*. Cloutier bought full-page ads in the *Hollywood Reporter* and in *Variety* to inform the entertainment world that *The René Simard*

Show was "the sensation of Canadian television." He even had Simard take an immersion course in English in Beverly Hills. If you're going to make it big in the U.S., you might as well learn to speak American.

The let's-do-it-the-American-way mentality that brought us *The René Simard Show* surfaced in other areas at the CBC too. For instance, I find the high jpm promos for upcoming items on *The National* extremely irritating. After all, even *Sesame Street* doesn't tell us what's coming next; it assumes we're hooked. American newscasts use promos to tell us what's coming *after* the commercials. But *The National* doesn't have commercials. So what's *its* excuse? And it's not just the promos. *The National*, wrote Robert Fulford, "opens every night with a graphic sequence so portentous that it could be justified only by the Apocalypse or at least the fall of the government. The news itself is inevitably an anti-climax." And *Venture*, a show about business, to judge by some of its early episodes, seems to have more in common with *Entertainment Tonight* than it does with the CBC tradition of magazine shows. As the Toronto *Star* said, *Venture* "took the viewers inside too many places at too fast and superficial a pace....The show's four pre-taped items...at times seemed to owe more in style to rock videos and *The A-Team* than television documentaries."

And it happens in drama too. At one point during John Hirsch's tenure as head of CBC drama, I was invited to try my hand at writing a television play. I chose as my form the docudrama, and as my subject Tim Buck, leader of the Canadian Communist Party, who, under the terms of the War Measures Act, was thrown in jail for four years in 1931. He and others were jailed not for anything they'd done, but just for being Communists. Canada thus became the first democracy to jail its Communist leaders. During Buck's time at Kingston penitentiary, there was a prison riot in which he did not take part but during which prison guards fired eight shots into his cell. This was at first denied by prison authorities, and only finally came to light during a Royal Commission inquiry into the riot.

I laboured mightily over my script but wasn't able to make it work. Finally, I asked the CBC if someone could help me. But at that time there were no story editors in the drama department. (A story editor is to TV drama what a pitching coach is to baseball.) The CBC brought in an expatriate Canadian from Hollywood to "fix" my script. Among other things, his revised version called for the "best special effects scene ever mounted on Canadian television" during the scene in which shots are fired into Buck's cell. The cell was to be blown to smithereens. That everyone — including the Royal Commission — would then know that something had happened in Buck's cell didn't occur to the fixer. He was too intent on raising the physical jpm level of the story. Emotional and intellectual jolts just weren't enough. Happily, the play was never produced.

Like American TV, and unlike the CBC at its best, Canadian private television is much higher in jpm's. Let's consider yet another difference between Canadian and American television.

The Difference in Mood and Tone

"We [Americans] prefer the glossy surface to the scarred interior." — Robert Brustein, *The New Republic*

I

There aren't just structural differences between Canadian and American television; there are also differences in mood, feeling and tone. Much of American television (and film) is about the American dream — the world as we wish it could be, a place in which goodness and reason prevail and things work out for the best. Much of Canadian television (and film), on the other hand, is about reality — the grey world as we actually find it.

American television tells lies — beautiful lies. For example, *Love Boat*, which appears on Global ("The *Love Boat* Network"), tells us that stories of true love always end happily. *The Waltons*, a programme which was also quite low in jpm's, told us every week for years that despite everything we'd heard about the Depression, it was really a lot of fun. If you were a close-knit family and spoke homilies all the time, no obstacle was too great to overcome. Canada's answer to *The Waltons* is the documentary realism of *Ten Lost Years*, as book, play and TV drama.

History on American commercial TV is almost always romanticized. No questions are asked that can't be answered. No loose ends are allowed to trouble the viewer.

What we get are the nice neat perspectives of adult fairy tales. Only rarely does one see on telelvision a programme that offers as complex a view of an historical event as does Marcel Ophuls in his splendid four-hour film about the German occupation of France, *The Sorrow and the Pity*. (To its everlasting credit, the English network of the CBC showed the film in an uncut, subtitled version in prime time in the mid-1970s.) The play *Sadat* on American TV turns the former Egyptian leader into a saint. But to make him look like a saint his domestic politics had to be ignored. *The Missiles of October*, about the stationing of Soviet missiles in Cuba, doesn't mention the Americans' secret agreement to withdraw their own missiles from Turkey. Americans, it seems, would rather not be told the truth. "Truth hurts," says a man in a Jules Feiffer cartoon. "Before truth, this was a happy country. But look what truth did to us in Vietnam! Look how truth fouled us up in the sixties and the seventies! Truth changed us from a nation of optimists to pessimists!"

In pursuit of the American dream, of trying to make things right everywhere, the U.S. sent 500,000 men to Vietnam. What Canadians do, on the other hand, is a lot of observing, whether as peacekeepers in Cyprus or as journalists in Vietnam. It's appropriate, therefore, that it was a Canadian-born journalist, Morley Safer of CBS, who in August 1965 first alerted American television viewers to some of the truth of what was happening in Vietnam. Safer showed U.S. marines setting fire to a peasant village with cigarette lighters; but all they succeeded in doing was capturing four bewildered old men. One angry viewer that night was President Lyndon Johnson. Informed that Safer wasn't a Communist, just a Canadian, Johnson replied, "Well, I knew he wasn't an American."

Another Canadian journalist, the CBC's Michael Maclear, became the only western correspondent to attend

Ho Chi Minh's funeral in 1969. One year later Maclear became the first reporter to interview American prisoners of war in North Vietnam. His interviews caused a sensation in the U.S. In 1980 Maclear and an independent Canadian production team pulled off another journalistic coup. They obtained exclusive access to film in Hanoi's military archives and succeeded in interviewing many of the participants on all sides of the conflict. Using footage from many other archives, and a script by New Zealand journalist Peter Arnett, they produced the fine series *The Ten Thousand Day War*. It consists of twenty-six half-hour programmes which begin in 1945, when Ho Chi Minh's army, having defeated the Japanese, turns its guns against France's returning colonial forces. The events that follow — Dien Bien Phu, the introduction of American advisors into South Vietnam, the assassination of Diem, the Gulf of Tonkin Resolution, My Lai, Khe Sanh, the Tet offensive, the bombing of Hanoi — all seem to lead inevitably to the North Vietnamese victory parade in Saigon and the dreadful plight of the boat people. The conspiracy view of history remains popular these days. I must confess that I subscribe to the stupidity view of history. Stupidity is a much underrated quality in human affairs — far more is wrought by bumblers than by conspirators. Michael Maclear's *The Ten Thousand Day War*, like Barbara Tuchman's *The March of Folly*, bears this out.

II

The documentary tradition, the tradition of telling it like it is, has been at the heart of Canadian film from its beginnings. John Grierson, who founded the National Film Board in 1939, is generally credited with having begun the Canadian documentary tradition. But that tradition predates Grierson. One need only recall the Moose River

play. Most of the demands made on the camera are
focus on tits, asses and cars. The characters are all so
reotypical that one doesn't really care about any of them.
nsequently there is no real tension. It's all too predict-
e. The dialogue is all right, I suppose, although many
the characters tend to sound the same. This is a film
an undiscriminating audience *anywhere*. There's noth-
particularly to commend it to a Canadian audience.
on't think the script is fixable. If the CFDC were to
port this film, I think I'd be tempted to shoot myself."
e CFDC phoned to ask me if I was kidding. I told them
asn't, and I was never asked again to read a script.)

III

documentary tradition has been at the centre of CBC
vision from its beginnings. It's been there in current
irs shows from *Close Up* to *the fifth estate* and in series
as *This Land*. And it's been there in the work of such
vidual producers as Cameron Graham and Donald
tain, whose TV programmes over the past couple of
des have helped create a past for large numbers of
adians who neither knew nor cared that they had one.
1967, Cameron Graham produced *Hail and Farewell*,
ignant ninety-minute documentary about John
enbaker's final days as leader of the Conservative
y. Who would have thought Canadian politics could
exciting, so moving? A year later, Graham produced
Style is the Man Himself, a ninety-minute *cinéma vérité*
ination of Pierre Trudeau's rise to power; this
ramme won a Canadian Film Award for Best Tele-
n Documentary of 1968. Three years later Graham
The Tenth Decade, an eight-hour series about the
enbaker-Pearson years.
1973, Cameron Graham completed his thirteen-part

mine disaster on radio. Or the extraordinary footage of
Newfoundland sealers, none of whom could swim, skipping from ice floe to ice floe in *The Viking* (1931) to be
reminded that the documentary form was alive and well
before Grierson set foot in Canada. The documentary
may be in our blood. Pierre Berton comments in *Why We
Act Like Canadians*: "As northerners we are better teachers
than entertainers. Our best films, our best radio, our best
television have been the kind that instructs and informs
as it entertains. The public affairs programme, the documentary, the serious classical drama — these are our
strengths."* I wish Berton had explored that point in more
detail.

The NFB's mandate, as set out under the Film Act, is
to "interpret Canada to Canadians and the rest of the
world." But the NFB has done more than interpret, says
Albert Kish, director of *The Image Makers*, a feature-length
film about the board. Kish argues that the NFB actually
"invented Canada." Before the NFB, "Canada was a far
away place to most of its citizens. It was through these
films that people [began to] see the country, understand
it and feel part of it."

At first there were documentaries about the importance
of winning the war, the *Canada Carries On* series, for

---

* Lawren Harris wrestled with the same question in the 1920s. "We
in Canada," he wrote in *The Canadian Theosophist*, "are in different
circumstances....Our population is sparse, the psychic atmosphere
is comparatively clean, whereas the States fill up and the masses
crowd a heavy psychic blanket over nearly all the land. We are on
the fringe of the great North and its living whiteness, its loneliness
and replenishment, its resignation and release, its call and answer
— its cleansing rhythms. It seems that the top of the continent is a
source of spiritual flow that will ever shed clarity into the growing
race of America, and we Canadians being closest to this source seem
destined to produce an art somewhat different from our Southern
fellows — an art more spacious, of a greater living quiet, perhaps
of a more certain conviction of eternal values."

example. Later there were documentaries about almost every aspect of Canadian life — its regions, its history, its people. By the 1960s, lightweight equipment made possible new kinds of documentary — such *cinéma vérité* successes as Pierre Perreault and Michel Brault's *Pour la suite du monde*. In the tradition of Robert Flaherty, *Pour la suite du monde* (1963) is a loving look at the people of Ile-aux-Coudres in the St. Lawrence as they attempt to revive the porpoise hunt of their ancestors.

It's not surprising that our narrative film tradition has also been strongly documentary. Certainly it was a natural step for the NFB to move from *Pour la suite du monde* to the improvised acting and dialogue of Donald Owen's *Nobody Waved Good-bye* (1964), a film about a young man who rebels against his family's middle-class values only to face an uncertain future. (Facing an uncertain future is what most of Canada's best narrative films are about — life as it is, rather than as we'd like it to be.) Another NFB film, Peter Pearson's *Best Damn Fiddler From Calabogie to Kaladar* (1968), also skilfully combines scripted material and actors with documentary footage and non-actors. It concerns the Prometers, a poor Ottawa Valley family who reject the attempts of middle-class social workers and doctors to make them conform.

Non-NFB feature films have the same realistic mood and tone. Paul Lynch's *The Hard Part Begins* (1974) is the story of a country and western singer, Donnelly Rhodes, who has been performing in pubs in small town Ontario for years while waiting for his big break. Like Ginger Coffey, he suddenly realizes that there isn't going to be a big break. This is it. (When the Americans make films about country and western singers — *Coalminer's Daughter* and *Tender Mercies* — they have happy endings. Otherwise they wouldn't get made.)

There isn't a better Canadian film than Michel Brault's

Les Ordres (1974), about the effect of the the War Measures Act on 5 of the 450 me arrested without reason and held with Although it's a scripted film, *Les Ordres* is documentary style. It's based on interview those who were imprisoned. By choosing the politics of the time, the film offers a what it's like to be a political prisoner. (Le had minimal theatrical distribution in Er has yet to be seen on English-Canadian te

The Canadian documentary tradition particularly popular with Canadians thems students much prefer the sugar-coated, version of life served up by the American to see real life, they say, they can go hang laundromat. They want to go to movies to not to be made to think or feel. For inher mentary is the notion that once people se are, they can understand them and may them.

(For a while in the late 1970s, Canadian in *Canadian* films led to an attempt to cr of Hollywood North. Canadian Film Corporation money and tax incentives enterprise along. At one point, the CFD to evaluate — *Middle Age Crazy*. I had n at the time that the film would be mad Bruce Dern and Ann Margret, and woul its way onto my Pay-TV screen. My r concluded: "This is an identity crisis fi isfactory resolution. The material is *not* film; it's far too thin. It might at best w

---

* I was once turned down for an Ontario Arts
Canadian films at the same time that a frien
another body to study why Canadian films a

1. Realism gives Canadian television much of its distinctiveness. An outstanding example was *Charlie Grant's War*, starring R.H. Thomson.

2. Who would have thought that a show about the romantic life of a United Farmers of Alberta candidate could draw more than 2,000,000 viewers? Terence Kelly and Janet Laine-Green in *Chautauqua Girl*.

3. Like *Dallas, Empire Inc.* was about power, money, sex and violence. But it also had character development.

4. Despite the likes of *Empire Inc.*, CBC drama is in decline. There was twice as much drama on the network in the 1950s and 1960s. Below, Larry Mann and Bruno Gerussi in *Louis Riel*.

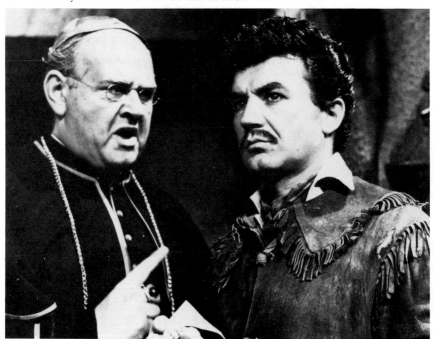

5.   A popular series of the 1960s was the political drama *Quentin Durgens, M.P.*, starring Gorden Pinsent. *Durgens* is just one example of a Canadian show for which there has been no U.S. equivalent.

6.   *Duplessis*, a dramatic portrayal of the mercurial Quebec politician's career, electrified French Canada. At one point, Duplessis (Jean Lapointe) remarks that half the people in the room — meaning the Liberal MNAs — are crooks. The Union Nationale leader is ordered to withdraw the statement. All right, says Duplessis, half the people in the room are *not* crooks.

7.   The two-headed nature of the CBC does little to ensure the two solitudes speak to each other. Like *Duplessis, Yesterday the Children Were Dancing* (with Gratien and Yves Gélinas) was a rare example of a production seen in both languages.

8.   Because we were slow establishing television archives in Canada, many early TV programmes were lost. Few episodes of the continuing drama of *The Plouffe Family*, for example, remain. Amanda Alari and Jean-Louis Roux are seen in a 1956 episode.

mine disaster on radio. Or the extraordinary footage of Newfoundland sealers, none of whom could swim, skipping from ice floe to ice floe in *The Viking* (1931) to be reminded that the documentary form was alive and well before Grierson set foot in Canada. The documentary may be in our blood. Pierre Berton comments in *Why We Act Like Canadians*: "As northerners we are better teachers than entertainers. Our best films, our best radio, our best television have been the kind that instructs and informs as it entertains. The public affairs programme, the documentary, the serious classical drama — these are our strengths."* I wish Berton had explored that point in more detail.

The NFB's mandate, as set out under the Film Act, is to "interpret Canada to Canadians and the rest of the world." But the NFB has done more than interpret, says Albert Kish, director of *The Image Makers*, a feature-length film about the board. Kish argues that the NFB actually "invented Canada." Before the NFB, "Canada was a far away place to most of its citizens. It was through these films that people [began to] see the country, understand it and feel part of it."

At first there were documentaries about the importance of winning the war, the *Canada Carries On* series, for

---

* Lawren Harris wrestled with the same question in the 1920s. "We in Canada," he wrote in *The Canadian Theosophist*, "are in different circumstances....Our population is sparse, the psychic atmosphere is comparatively clean, whereas the States fill up and the masses crowd a heavy psychic blanket over nearly all the land. We are on the fringe of the great North and its living whiteness, its loneliness and replenishment, its resignation and release, its call and answer — its cleansing rhythms. It seems that the top of the continent is a source of spiritual flow that will ever shed clarity into the growing race of America, and we Canadians being closest to this source seem destined to produce an art somewhat different from our Southern fellows — an art more spacious, of a greater living quiet, perhaps of a more certain conviction of eternal values."

example. Later there were documentaries about almost every aspect of Canadian life — its regions, its history, its people. By the 1960s, lightweight equipment made possible new kinds of documentary — such *cinéma vérité* successes as Pierre Perreault and Michel Brault's *Pour la suite du monde*. In the tradition of Robert Flaherty, *Pour la suite du monde* (1963) is a loving look at the people of Ile-aux-Coudres in the St. Lawrence as they attempt to revive the porpoise hunt of their ancestors.

It's not surprising that our narrative film tradition has also been strongly documentary. Certainly it was a natural step for the NFB to move from *Pour la suite du monde* to the improvised acting and dialogue of Donald Owen's *Nobody Waved Good-bye* (1964), a film about a young man who rebels against his family's middle-class values only to face an uncertain future. (Facing an uncertain future is what most of Canada's best narrative films are about — life as it is, rather than as we'd like it to be.) Another NFB film, Peter Pearson's *Best Damn Fiddler From Calabogie to Kaladar* (1968), also skilfully combines scripted material and actors with documentary footage and non-actors. It concerns the Prometers, a poor Ottawa Valley family who reject the attempts of middle-class social workers and doctors to make them conform.

Non-NFB feature films have the same realistic mood and tone. Paul Lynch's *The Hard Part Begins* (1974) is the story of a country and western singer, Donnelly Rhodes, who has been performing in pubs in small town Ontario for years while waiting for his big break. Like Ginger Coffey, he suddenly realizes that there isn't going to be a big break. This is it. (When the Americans make films about country and western singers — *Coalminer's Daughter* and *Tender Mercies* — they have happy endings. Otherwise they wouldn't get made.)

There isn't a better Canadian film than Michel Brault's

Les Ordres (1974), about the effect of the imposition of the War Measures Act on 5 of the 450 men and women arrested without reason and held without charge. Although it's a scripted film, *Les Ordres* is presented in a documentary style. It's based on interviews with fifty of those who were imprisoned. By choosing not to focus on the politics of the time, the film offers a chilling look at what it's like to be a political prisoner. (*Les Ordres*, which had minimal theatrical distribution in English Canada, has yet to be seen on English-Canadian television.)

The Canadian documentary tradition has never been particularly popular with Canadians themselves.* My film students much prefer the sugar-coated, larger-than-life version of life served up by the Americans. If they want to see real life, they say, they can go hang out at the local laundromat. They want to go to movies to be entertained, not to be made to think or feel. For inherent in the documentary is the notion that once people see things as they are, they can understand them and maybe even change them.

(For a while in the late 1970s, Canadian's lack of interest in *Canadian* films led to an attempt to create here a kind of Hollywood North. Canadian Film Development Corporation money and tax incentives helped the whole enterprise along. At one point, the CFDC sent me a script to evaluate — *Middle Age Crazy*. I had no way of knowing at the time that the film would be made, and would star Bruce Dern and Ann Margret, and would eventually make its way onto my Pay-TV screen. My report on the film concluded: "This is an identity crisis film with an unsatisfactory resolution. The material is *not* suited to a feature film; it's far too thin. It might at best work as a one-hour

---

* I was once turned down for an Ontario Arts Council grant to show Canadian films at the same time that a friend was given a grant by another body to study why Canadian films are so rarely seen.

TV play. Most of the demands made on the camera are to focus on tits, asses and cars. The characters are all so stereotypical that one doesn't really care about any of them. Consequently there is no real tension. It's all too predictable. The dialogue is all right, I suppose, although many of the characters tend to sound the same. This is a film for an undiscriminating audience *anywhere*. There's nothing particularly to commend it to a Canadian audience. I don't think the script is fixable. If the CFDC were to support this film, I think I'd be tempted to shoot myself." The CFDC phoned to ask me if I was kidding. I told them I wasn't, and I was never asked again to read a script.)

III

The documentary tradition has been at the centre of CBC television from its beginnings. It's been there in current affairs shows from *Close Up* to *the fifth estate* and in series such as *This Land*. And it's been there in the work of such individual producers as Cameron Graham and Donald Brittain, whose TV programmes over the past couple of decades have helped create a past for large numbers of Canadians who neither knew nor cared that they had one.

In 1967, Cameron Graham produced *Hail and Farewell*, a poignant ninety-minute documentary about John Diefenbaker's final days as leader of the Conservative Party. Who would have thought Canadian politics could be so exciting, so moving? A year later, Graham produced *The Style is the Man Himself*, a ninety-minute *cinéma vérité* examination of Pierre Trudeau's rise to power; this programme won a Canadian Film Award for Best Television Documentary of 1968. Three years later Graham made *The Tenth Decade*, an eight-hour series about the Diefenbaker-Pearson years.

In 1973, Cameron Graham completed his thirteen-part

1. Realism gives Canadian television much of its distinctiveness. An outstanding example was *Charlie Grant's War*, starring R.H. Thomson.

2. Who would have thought that a show about the romantic life of a United Farmers of Alberta candidate could draw more than 2,000,000 viewers? Terence Kelly and Janet Laine-Green in *Chautauqua Girl*.

3. Like *Dallas*, *Empire Inc.* was about power, money, sex and violence. But it also had character development.

4. Despite the likes of *Empire Inc.*, CBC drama is in decline. There was twice as much drama on the network in the 1950s and 1960s. Below, Larry Mann and Bruno Gerussi in *Louis Riel*.

5.   A popular series of the 1960s was the political drama *Quentin Durgens, M.P.*, starring Gorden Pinsent. *Durgens* is just one example of a Canadian show for which there has been no U.S. equivalent.

6.   *Duplessis*, a dramatic portrayal of the mercurial Quebec politician's career, electrified French Canada. At one point, Duplessis (Jean Lapointe) remarks that half the people in the room — meaning the Liberal MNAs — are crooks. The Union Nationale leader is ordered to withdraw the statement. All right, says Duplessis, half the people in the room are *not* crooks.

7.   The two-headed nature of the CBC does little to ensure the two solitudes speak to each other. Like *Duplessis*, *Yesterday the Children Were Dancing* (with Gratien and Yves Gélinas) was a rare example of a production seen in both languages.

8.   Because we were slow establishing television archives in Canada, many early TV programmes were lost. Few episodes of the continuing drama of *The Plouffe Family*, for example, remain. Amanda Alari and Jean-Louis Roux are seen in a 1956 episode.

9. "Regional" programming has been largely absent on the CBC. An authentic regional programme, *Don Messer's Jubilee*, was cancelled because CBC executives in central Canada found it embarrassingly provincial. Instead we got René Simard — from British Columbia.

10. As of the fall of 1985, Canadian children could no longer gather round the castle hearth to be entertained by the Friendly Giant (Bob Homme), Jerome and Rusty. This fine example of Canadian children's programming disappeared during a flurry of cutbacks.

11. In Canada, the dominant comic form has been satire. Wayne and Shuster, seen here in their famous Shakespearean baseball skit, have been followed by the Royal Canadian Air Farce, SCTV and the Frantics.

12. SCTV, which began on Ontario's Global network in the mid-1970s, was not only funny, it literally "destroyed" television. Joe Flaherty and John Candy were two members of the talented cast.

13. *King of Kensington* demonstrated that it was possible to take an American form — the sitcom — and do something distinctively Canadian with it. With star Al Waxman are producers Louis del Grande and Jack Humphrey.

14. After the success of *King of Kensington*, Louis del Grande went to Hollywood. He discovered, to his surprise, that he hated it there. He returned to Canada and created the unique series *Seeing Things*, in which he stars with Martha Gibson.

15. *Front Page Challenge* started out as an attempt to imitate glitzy American game shows. But the flashing lights, buzzers and beautiful models soon gave way to an unadorned mixture of quick thinking and current affairs that has proved as durable as *Hockey Night in Canada*.

16. As first chairman of the CRTC, Pierre Juneau presided over the first stages of the undermining of the CBC's central role in Canadian broadcasting. Now, ironically, Juneau is president of the CBC.

TV autobiography of Lester B. Pearson, *First Person Singular*. That series of half-hour programmes is much more satisfying as autobiography than the three volumes of Pearson memoirs prepared by the University of Toronto Press. The books, unfortunately, aren't really memoirs since they consist for the most part of others saying what they *think* Pearson would have said. *First Person Singular*, although a far from complete document, at least has the advantage of presenting us with Pearson's own voice and words.

Unlike Lester Pearson, John Diefenbaker wasn't an historian; he was an anecdotalist — more entertaining to listen to than Pearson, but much more difficult to keep on track. That presented the producer of a programme such as *One Canadian* (1975) with special difficulties. Whereas much of the footage in Pearson's *First Person Singular* narrated itself and seems to have needed little editing, Diefenbaker had to be questioned closely, and even then it took a great deal of juggling in the editing room to get the chronology straight. That resulted — particularly in the early shows in *One Canadian* — in a choppy format. Nevertheless, Graham makes it work.

A variety of John Diefenbakers flit across the screen. The Diefenbaker who's insecure, the one who looks almost like a little boy as he searches the faces around him for approval, whether he's just caught a fish or spoken what he thinks is a clever line. The Diefenbaker who uses the English language unlike any other Canadian politician. (It's not only his use of words like "ilk," "anathema," "excoriate," and "orchidaceous," but his outrageous constructions such as his description of Marcel Faribault's *deux nations* proposal as a "ferryboat to extinction.") The Diefenbaker who's not above stretching the truth in support of his image as civil libertarian. He claims that although his fellow Conservatives supported the deportation of Japanese-Canadians in 1942, he opposed it. Perhaps he did, but his opposition isn't on record. The Diefenbaker who is mean-spirited; his contempt for George Hees knows no bounds. The Diefenbaker who comes from Prince Albert. Those of us who've grown up in central Canada will never really be able to understand the devotion of his constituents and of the West generally. Finally, the Diefenbaker who moves me to tears every time I see the shots of him lurching out of his seat at Maple Leaf Gardens in 1967 to applaud the announcement that the new leader of the Conservative Party is Robert Stanfield.

It's not surprising that the picture John Diefenbaker sets out to give us of John Diefenbaker in *One Canadian* is a highly flattering one. They're his memoirs, and he has to be able to tell the story his way. Cameron Graham has done a superb job of helping him tell that story. The result is that, as in the case of Pearson, Diefenbaker's television memoirs are superior to his literary ones.

The great strength of Cameron Graham's work at its best is its simplicity of form. In the world of TV documentary-making, he remains a traditionalist. Graham has little or no interest in re-enactments of history à la *The National Dream* or some of the segments of *The October Crisis*. He works with the actual documents and with people who were there: still photographs; short, carefully chosen film clips; quotations from *Hansard* or elsewhere; lots of people just talking into the camera; a narrator or interviewer to tie it all together; and a good, original musical score. There's not much fancy stuff in a Graham documentary.

Donald Brittain's approach to documentary has been less respectful, more ironic than that of Cameron Graham. If Graham sees politics as high drama, Brittain sees it as melodrama. Brittain tells the story of being in Washington in the fall of 1963 trying to persuade White House officials to permit him to film a day in the life of John F. Kennedy. While discussions about the film were going on, Brittain was permitted to observe the White House in action. He was taken into the Oval Office, where a friendly, smiling Kennedy sat talking to a French official. Relations between France and the U.S. were at a low point that fall and a senior French diplomat had come to Washington to discuss the matter. Some TV cameramen were ushered into the room. As soon as the TV lights went on, Kennedy stopped smiling and looked angry until the picture-taking had ended. Then he went back to being as warm and friendly as he'd been before the cameras arrived. Brittain never got to make his film; Kennedy was assassinated that fall. But if his film had been made, it would undoubtedly have included such material, not as a way of making fun of Kennedy or of politics, but to demonstrate that politics is partly showbusiness and that a constant awareness of that is crucial to its understanding.

Brittain's sensibility often brings us fresh perspectives on familiar material. His two-hour CBC/NFB documentary *The Champions* (1978), about the parallel careers of Pierre Trudeau and René Lévesque, presented us with few facts we weren't already aware of, and little footage many of us hadn't seen before. Nonetheless, *The Champions* helped us to understand the two men and their time more clearly. In the larger perspective, we saw that Pierre Trudeau treated the media with precisely the same disdain in the 1960s as he did in the 1970s. What had changed was not Trudeau but us; what we accepted in him then had come to seem mean and arrogant. Jean Marchand comes across as a much more interesting and important figure than the rather comic and inept one he'd become for many of us by the late 1970s. In 1949 he politicizes his dilettantish friend Pierre Trudeau by getting him involved in the Asbestos Strike. A decade later he does the same thing to a reluctant René Lévesque during a producers' strike at the CBC. *The Champions* shows us a lovable René Lévesque. He goes to a Grey Cup game and sits there shivering, confused by the rules. In a playful gesture reminiscent of Chaplin, he reaches out and caresses Pierre Trudeau's fur coat. But the film also shows us a vindictive Lévesque. On the night of his election in 1960, at the beginning of Quebec's Quiet Revolution, Lévesque insists on personally ensuring that a restaurateur he'd been feuding with, and whose licence he'd threatened to revoke, has been shut down.

There are, of course, other producers who are doing documentary work that is equally distinguished. John Zaritsky produced the ninety-minute, Academy Award winning *Just Another Missing Kid* (1981), about the murder of a young Ottawa man, for *the fifth estate*. His independently produced *I'll Get There Somehow* (1985) tells of four tough women and their continuing battle with arthritis. Two of them have rheumatoid arthritis. A third has osteoarthritis. The fourth, a victim of lupus, the most deadly form of the disease, devotes her time to helping others fight back.

And there's the John McGreevy series *Cities*, independently produced in conjunction with Nielsen-Ferns and screened by the CBC. The idea was to get articulate, well known people talking in a personal way about cities that are, or have been, important to them. The result is, for the most part, a delight. The one Canadian city in the series was *Glenn Gould's Toronto*. Although Gould was from Toronto (and continued to live there until his death) he was not really *of* Toronto. His nocturnal habits — to say nothing of his agoraphobia — meant that he had literally *never* seen most of the city. Much of what he shares with us in this film, he's experiencing for the first time himself.

That's part of the fun. Zipping up the outside of the CN Tower in an elevator, listening to Glenn Gould playing Strauss, is a wonderful example of what Susan Sontag would call "radical juxtaposition." Says Gould, "They tell me that from up there on a clear day you can see, if not forever, at least Buffalo." We ride down another elevator with Gould, this time in the monstrous Eaton Centre. The Hallelujah Chorus sounds in the background. Gould shakes his head incredulously, commenting, "I don't believe it. It's absurd. It's absolutely absurd. Some people say this is Toronto's answer to the Galleria in Milan. Whether that's true or not, it sure ain't your average Ma and Pa Kettle corner store." We drive with Gould through one of Toronto's suburbs — the kind we're all supposed to hate — and he tells us, without a trace of irony: "This I think represents the North American suburban dream at its very best, and I love it." Perhaps the most memorable moment in the film occurs when Gould sings a Mahler *lied* to some elephants at the Toronto zoo. The elephants begin to edge nervously away.

IV

Many of our best dramatic programmes and series also reflect the documentary tradition. We have turned necessity into a virtue. In 1969, Britain's *Radio Times* introduced the CBC series *Wojeck* to a British audience this way: "Lack of studios, the fact that acting talent couldn't be retained — it tended to drain away to New York and Hollywood — led [Canadians] to specialise in the documentary. The pioneering National Film Board supplied a powerful amount of support and encouragement.... Pure documentary led on to dramatised documentary, usually with a strong current of social comment. Some notable examples, such as *Nobody Waved Goodbye* have been seen on

BBC-tv. And now *Wojeck*, made on location using documentary techniques." *Wojeck* is about a Toronto coroner's obsessive need to find out how and why people died. The stories, though fictional, are based on reality. In *The Last Man in the World*, for example, Steve Wojeck looks into the circumstances surrounding the death of a Cree Indian who has committed suicide in a city jail. Wojeck knows how he died, but insists on knowing why it was allowed to happen.

The CBC's *For the Record* series also explores stories behind newspaper headlines. The award-winning *Ready for Slaughter* is about a fourth generation Ontario beef farmer threatened by the economic realities of the 1980s. "This isn't my job," cries the farmer, played by Gordon Pinsent. "It's my life. You're taking my life from me." Finally he realizes that the only way he and other farmers can take on the banks is to organize. But he has to give up some of his conservative, independent ways. *Ready for Slaughter* could have turned into an earnest political tract — as many *For the Record* episodes do — but a good script by Roy MacGregor and understated direction by Allan King ensured the play's success.

Or consider Imperial Oil's seven-part *Newcomers* series shown by the CBC in 1979. Especially the Irish episode. In 1847, Ireland was ravaged by a potato famine in which a million people died. Half a million others fled the country on crowded, cholera-ridden boats. Many thousands perished on these "floating coffins" and were buried at sea; tens of thousands of others were forcibly detained in quarantine camps when they arrived in North America. A small plaque on Grosse Ile in the St. Lawrence still reads: "In this secluded spot lie the mortal remains of 5424 persons who, fleeing from pestilence and famine in Ireland in the year 1847, found in America but a grave."

I had a vague, textbook knowledge of the story of these

immigrants before I saw the *1847* episode of *Newcomers*. It's one thing to read about such events, quite another to see them well dramatized. And that, of course, was the value of this generally fine series, which helped put into a larger perspective an experience almost all of us share — we either are immigrants or are descended from them. *The Newcomers*, by showing us what it might have been like to be an immigrant from France in 1740, or Scotland in 1832, or Ireland in 1847, or Denmark in 1911, or the Ukraine in 1927, or Italy in 1949, made a significant contribution to Canadian social history.

In *1847*, Irish men and women who've been lucky enough to survive their ghastly trip arrive in Upper Canada only to be greeted by signs placed by Scottish and English immigrants: "No Irish or Dogs" and "Blacksmith's Helper Wanted: No Irish Need Apply." (Seventy-five years later my Polish-Jewish parents were welcomed by signs announcing NO DOGS OR JEWS ALLOWED. Some of the signs *they* found were no doubt placed there by descendants of the Irish immigrants of 1847.)

Or there's my favourite, the seven-part *Duplessis* series. Maurice Duplessis, the former premier of Quebec, became a non-person almost immediately after his death in 1959. By the time a ten-foot bronze statue of Duplessis had been delivered to Quebec City in 1961, Jean Lesage and the Liberals were in power and a royal commission was investigating Duplessis. Lesage, and public works minister René Lévesque, didn't know what to do with the statue. They tried to give it to Poland along with some Polish art treasures that were being returned. But it turned out the bronze in the statue was classified as a semi-strategic material; it was illegal to give Duplessis to an Iron Curtain country. The statue was hidden away.

Not until almost a decade and a half after his death did things begin to change. In 1972, the brilliant French-

Canadian director Denys Arcand produced a three-hour NFB documentary, *Québec: Duplessis et après*, which explored the extent to which Duplessis's influence lived on in Quebec. In 1973, Robert Rumilly's sympathetic biography, *Maurice Duplessis et son temps*, was published and René Lévesque, now head of the Parti Québécois, began to speak admiringly of Duplessis. It was Maurice Duplessis, Lévesque announced, who had started Quebec on the road to independence. The celebrations that occurred when the P.Q. came to power in 1976 were like nothing Quebec had seen since Duplessis himself had driven the corrupt Taschereau Liberals from office forty years earlier. In 1977, when the P.Q. finally unveiled the Duplessis statue, leaders of the P.Q. and Union Nationale competed to see who could say the nicest things about the old man. Then a French translation of a biography of Duplessis by Conrad Black became one of the biggest-selling works of Canadian non-fiction to be published in Quebec in twenty years.

In the winter of 1978, Duplessis's resurrection was made complete with the presentation of a superb seven-part TV biography on the French-language CBC. As usual, the two separate but equal networks that make up the CBC made no provision in planning and preparing *Duplessis* for it to be seen by all Canadians. *Duplessis* wasn't screened by the English-language network until 1984, and then in abbreviated (four-hour) dubbed and subtitled versions. The series was conceived and directed by Mark Blandford, who had produced *The October Crisis* (1975) and *Empire Inc.* Every Wednesday for seven weeks more than two million Quebeckers sat down to another episode of *Duplessis*; except for the Canada-Russia hockey series of 1972, more people watched the programmes than had ever watched anything on French-Canadian television. Television critics hailed *Duplessis* as a kind of French-Canadian *Roots*. "Jamais la télé n'a si bien parlé de nous," read one headline.

Denys Arcand's script, based on official documents, correspondence, newspaper articles and reminiscences, offers us an excellent backroom look at Duplessis. This is not the Duplessis of *Charbonneau et le chef* or *The Roncarelli Affair*. It's the view a not unsympathetic observer might have. Although the series presents Duplessis as a compelling and sympathetic figure, it's certainly no whitewash. He becomes premier as a result of his campaign against the corruption of Taschereau's Liberals; but as premier he himself employs a full-time "fund-raiser" whose job it is to collect ten per cent of all government contracts — in cash — for the Union Nationale. According to the series, none of that money was used to line anyone's pockets. Duplessis himself died $40,000 in debt.

Jean Lapointe — familiar to us as the photographer in *J.A. Martin, photographe* and the cab driver in *Les Ordres* — is an excellent Duplessis. Like *le chef*, Lapointe contains multitudes. He's tough, coarse, devious, loyal, solitary — and incapable of being any of those things in moderation. When he gives up his addiction to alcohol in 1942, he takes up drinking gallons of orange juice instead. He's a workaholic whose only holidays are trips to the World Series, where he feeds his addiction to sports statistics. Duplessis is surprisingly funny. At one point, as opposition leader sitting on the public accounts committee, he remarks that half the people in the room — meaning the Liberal members of the committee — are crooks. The chairman orders him to withdraw the remark. All right, says Duplessis, half the people in the room are *not* crooks.

IV

Sometimes, like the Americans, we too succumb to the temptation to tell beautiful lies. James Murray and Eric Till's eight-hour television series *The National Dream* (1974), for instance, was, like Pierre Berton's book, so intent on mythologizing the building of the CPR that the question of whether we really needed to build the railway when we did isn't dealt with.

Or take Nancy Ryley's two-part series about the Group of Seven, *The Passionate Canadians* (1977). The Group of Seven has always been surrounded by beautiful lies: that there were no European or Canadian precedents for their work; that they sprang almost full-blown from nowhere; that, having sprung, they were condemned by imperceptive critics like *Saturday Night*'s Hector Charlesworth. The first full-length study of the group, F.B. Housser's hagiography, *A Canadian Art Movement: The Story of the Group of Seven* (1926), was the source of much of this mythology. Only in recent years, with the publication of such books as Paul Duval's *Group of Seven Drawings* (1965) and Peter Mellen's *The Group of Seven* (1970) have some of the myths about the Group been debunked. We learned from Duval that landscape drawings of a "markedly Canadian character" had been done as early as 1893 by the Toronto Art Students' League; that in 1904, J.E.H. MacDonald of the Art Students' League had gone to Europe and steeped himself in art nouveau; that it was a marriage between art nouveau and landscape that had created the style of the Group of Seven. Peter Mellen pointed out that the Group had been far more often praised than condemned. Even old Hector Charlesworth had on occasion written admiringly of their work.

The Passionate Canadians wasn't on the screen for more than two minutes before it was clear that what we were getting was not the revised story of the Group as told by Mellen, Duval and others, but rather the earlier, romanticized version of the story. Narrator Harry Adaskin's overblown script speaks of the "herculean" and "thankless" task the Group undertook as they "battled with the critics for acceptance." Hector Charlesworth is portrayed as someone incapable of getting dressed, let alone knowing a good painting. Ryley has MacDonald proclaim in the middle of northern Ontario, "Canada doesn't look like England or Europe. It's ridiculous to go on imposing their ways of seeing on our own landscape. What we have to do is to paint it in a new way even if everyone thinks we're crazy." Lawren Harris awkwardly replies, "It's only through the arts that we can bring our environment into focus and begin to create a cultural tradition of our own." Given lines like these, it's not surprising that the acting in *The Passionate Canadians* is rarely more than wooden. Apart from a hint that Varley liked women, the Group is depicted as saintly.

Harry Rasky is another CBC producer who can't resist the temptation to tell beautiful lies. His *Homage to Chagall* suggests that the painter's work is about love. But, truth to tell, Marc Chagall's work is also about despair, fear and death. Why are those themes muted in Rasky's film? Rasky's film *Tennessee Williams' South* offers us a view of the playwright's home territory that's far too romanticized. The film may reflect the mellow mood Williams was in when it was shot, but where is the South that Williams himself had elsewhere described as "dragon country"? Surely it belongs in this film too. In *Arthur Miller on Home Ground* (1979), Rasky suggests that we're seeing and hearing a great man. But the sad fact, at least to judge by this film, is that Miller really has nothing to say over and above what his plays say. Miller comes across as an astonishingly inarticulate man constantly getting tangled in his syntax and banalities. "My work is, if I could write really about stuff that never went through me, I would probably write a play every two months but let's say three a year or two a year or something like that. I can think of innumerable terrific subjects, but I have no real, I didn't live them, somebody else lived them and I, it's not my business to write about them." Arthur Miller is living proof that an author or artist is often the worst person to ask about his or her own work.

V

On the other side of the blindly idealistic American coin I've been describing lie cynicism and despair. A lot of American programmes aren't just more violent and sensational than Canadian programmes, they're also more sleazy and misanthropic. I've already talked about the pessimistic tone of the old *Bob Newhart Show*. Its producers also created *Buffalo Bill*, a sitcom about a despicable talk show host. "His lone redeeming feature," wrote *Time* magazine, "is his unredeemability." There has been no Canadian equivalent of *Buffalo Bill*. And there have been no Canadian equivalents of such U.S. programmes as *Queen for a Day* and *The Gong Show*, programmes that by focusing on losers allow the rest of us to feel, temporarily, superior.

For ten years, beginning in the 1950s, *Queen for a Day* capitalized on human misery. Each day five women told their real-life hard-luck stories and explained why it was they needed a fridge or false teeth or whatever. Then, based on audience applause as measured by an applause-meter, the most wretched was crowned queen for a day and showered with gifts. Howard Blake, sometime producer of the series, said, "Sure, *Queen* was vulgar and sleazy and filled with bathos and bad taste. That was why it was so successful: it was exactly what the general public wanted."

The Gong Show in the late 1970s made *Queen for a Day* look almost respectable. Its host, Chuck ("Chuckie Baby") Barris, creator of such other misanthropic delights as *The Dating Game*, *The Newlywed Game* and *The $1.98 Beauty*

Show, was the very embodiment of sleaze. He hustled around the stage, always with a mocking sneer, saying: "We do hope we're whiling away some of those hours of quiet desperation." The looks on the faces of the contestants on *The Gong Show* as they were being subjected to the humiliating jibes of host and rowdy panel, who judged which of their performances was least awful, were a fascinating study in sado-masochism. The contestants, a man who blew a trumpet through his navel, a woman who stood on her head on a cup and spun slowly around while playing "Old Folks at Home" on the mandolin, knew exactly what they were letting themselves in for when they agreed to accept their few minutes of fame on TV. And yet you could see some of them flinch when they heard cruel things being said about them.

It's not just nonentities who choose to humiliate themselves on television programmes like *The Gong Show* or *People's Court*. Celebrities on talk shows compete to out-confess one another. Brooke Hayward has said of her experience, "Having revealed myself in a *controlled* way [in her book, *Haywire*], I found the idea of going out and publicizing myself disgusting. But then in a perverse way I began to enjoy it. Questions repeated over and over forced me to reveal more and more....I'm public property now." Or you get the pathetic Orson Welles, everybody's favourite failed genius, now reduced to the talk-show circuit.

Most of us work at jobs that don't challenge us; we spend much of our time with people we don't like. In response we cultivate an ironic detachment which allows us to be present and not present at the same time. As a result, nothing really seems to matter. Rose K. Goldsen writes in *The Show and Tell Machine*, "Wax build-up on the kitchen floor or a daughter who has been kidnapped — both are equally soul-wrenching to Mary Hartman. No matter what the problem, it's dealt with in the same flat, emotionless manner."

Ironic detachment characterized Tom Snyder, host of an NBC late-night programme. It didn't matter whether the subject was the fate of western civilization or hangnails — everything was discussed in the same cool, uninvolved way. Out come four performers who've had plastic surgery to make them look like Elvis Presley, Jim Croce, Jim Morrison and Janis Joplin. They tell us that having their faces permanently remade is no different from an actor putting on makeup to play a part. Snyder doesn't push the point. Out comes a man to discuss the implications for freedom of the press if he publishes the formula for building a homemade H-bomb. Out comes a singing chiropractor. It's all the same. The ultimate in democracy. Is it any wonder that we find it harder to make distinctions between what is serious and what is trivial? Try to explain to a starving Ethiopian the humour involved in having David Letterman (Snyder's successor) drop food from a five-storey tower so we can see how big a mess it makes. Eggs, tomatoes, watermelons are dropped and cameras zoom in to show us the effect.

VII

Happily, there are no Canadian counterparts to these programmes. The other side of the coin of Canadian realism is satire, the kind of satire provided by *Wayne and Shuster*, *SCTV*, and other shows. When I was a kid in the late 1940s, I looked forward to 9:30 on Thursday evenings when Wayne and Shuster's radio programme came on. Sometimes I even got tickets and went down to the studio at 21 McGill in Toronto to watch the show live. The first bit of material I ever plagiarized was from Wayne and Shuster. I used it in a skit in grade eight. A guy pounds on the door of a building shouting, "Is this the Hall of Medicine?" An irritated voice answers, "Yes! Who in the Hall do you want?"

I remember with pleasure Wayne and Shuster's early appearances on CBC television and how excited we all were in 1958 when Ed Sullivan signed them to appear as regulars on his show. The Toronto *Star* made the story front-page news. Wayne and Shuster were a sensation in the U.S; they even won a couple of awards as outstanding entertainers of the year.

The sophisticated sketches in the Jack Benny tradition that Wayne and Shuster did in those days had a spark to them that, for me, were second only to the material on Sid Caesar's *Your Show of Shows*. And Sid Caesar had the best comedy writers in America working for him. Wayne and Shuster did it all themselves. Their literate slapstick was a sheer delight. I remember with pleasure their take-off "The Brown Pumpernickel." "Sharpen your blade," says Robespierre to the keeper of the guillotine. "Tonight you'll be slicing Pumpernickel."

Those years — the late 1950s — were Wayne and Shuster's best; they were at the top of their form. To ensure that my often unreliable memory hasn't simply been playing tricks on me, I've looked at old kinescopes again. Those shows *are* as good as I remember. And in those days they were performing not only on the CBC but on Sullivan's show and on the BBC. They even wrote a regular newspaper column.

Wayne and Shuster haven't been the same since. One turning point in their career seemed to come with *Holiday Lodge*, a disastrous thirteen-week sitcom which replaced the Jack Benny programme on CBS in the summer of 1961. It was the only show they'd been involved with that they hadn't written themselves. Another turning point was the arrival of videotape in the early 1960s. Videotape meant Wayne and Shuster didn't have to go live; they could tape their shows and use a laugh track. A third turning point occurred in 1968 when they let it be known that they were available to do TV commercials if the money was right. Enter Gulf Oil. Around the same time, Wayne and Shuster's relations with the press turned sour. They'd been getting a lot of bad reviews and they lashed out, describing the press as "malicious."

In the past decade or more, I've stopped watching much of Wayne and Shuster because I haven't found them funny. Compared with the old days, Wayne and Shuster appear to be merely going through the motions; some vital spark is gone. TV overexposure is hard on some comedians: look at what happened to Milton Berle. Other comedians get burned out. Look at Sid Caesar and Imogene Coca. Whatever the reason in Wayne and Shuster's case, it's clear that they don't write as well or act as well as they did. In the late 1950s their scripts, their acting, their timing were so good that they could deliberately telegraph lines and situations and still make them work. There's a much more self-conscious quality to their work now. Much of what's good still occurs in updated versions of earlier successes. A repeat of the Shakespearean baseball game, for example. ("So fair a foul I have not seen.") Frequently their shows are best when they're not on the screen themselves. Their takeoffs on TV commercials are excellent.

Wayne and Shuster have had a long and successful run — longer than any other TV comedians. They've given us some of the funniest television many of us have seen. But I wonder if the time hasn't come for them to retire as performers and take on new roles. We've done a lousy job in this country of training writers, producers and directors of TV comedy. Who better to pass on some of the skills they've spent a lifetime in show business learning than Wayne and Shuster?

In recent years, we've had the brilliant satire of SCTV — most of it, regrettably, not on the CBC. (When SCTV came on the scene in the mid-1970s, the CBC gave them a bureaucratic run-around, and ABC's Fred Silverman declared they were "far too intelligent" for network distribution. Consequently, SCTV signed with Global and went into syndication. Only later did the show come to CBC.) One wonders whether SCTV would have burned out as quickly as it did had it been doing monthly specials for the CBC rather than ninety-minute weekly shows on NBC. Certainly Wayne and Shuster might have offered them some valuable advice on the subject.

Still, we have to be grateful for what we did get from SCTV (and much of it can still be seen in re-runs). There hasn't been a better send-up of television since the 1950s when Ernie Kovacs brought us *You Asked to See It*, Percy Dovetonsils, Mr. Question Man, and Clowdy Faire, Your Weather Girl. Thirty years from now I suspect we'll remember Andrea Martin as Edith Prickley, a kind of cross, according to the *Village Voice*, between Lina Wertmuller and Ann Landers; commercials for the Evelyn Woods Speed-Talking School; John Candy, cigarette and drink in hand, as Johnny LaRue, fitness instructor; *The Sammy Maudlin Show*; Bob and Doug Mackenzie; Joe Flaherty, host of *Monster Chiller Horror Theatre*; Dave Thomas as Walter Cronkite, host of *Dialing for Dollars*. Best of all were some take-offs on Canadian television. An SCTV version of *Goin' Down the Road. The Journal* with a pushy Barbara Frum being brushed off by an angry Colonel Qaddafi; he yells at her, "I'm being interviewed by Ted Koppel!".

Canadian television tends to be more realistic (and satirical), American more idealistic (and cynical). In the next chapter we'll see that the original establishment of public broadcasting in Canada was itself a function of Canadian realism.

Where We Are and How We Got Here

"We have succeeded in our essential national goal — that of creating an alternative way of being North American."
— Richard Gwyn

I

What's clear, I hope, is that there *is* a difference between Canadian and American culture. And that difference can be seen as clearly as any place on our TV screens. American commercial television, for the most part, aims at the lowest common denominator in its audience; Canadian public television, on the other hand, aims higher.

The irony is that although there is a difference, a difference that reflects who we are, we the viewers reject that image most of the time. We don't want to look into the mirror the CBC holds up to us. Instead, we spend eighty per cent of our viewing time watching American TV. (Children spend even more.) We prefer its fast pace and its beautiful lies. Life, after all, is difficult, and the last thing we want to do when we turn to television is to face reality. We want to escape it, and the fact is that Americans are the best in the world at producing escapist fare. As T.S. Eliot wrote, "Human kind/Cannot bear very much reality."

The irony is that we notice that CBC radio is distinctively different from American (and Canadian) commercial radio, and we praise the CBC for that, but we have much more difficulty seeing that a similar difference can be found on television. That difference remains invisible to most Canadians. We commend PBS for the quality of many of its programmes, but forget that one of the reasons public television exists at all in the U.S. is that Americans living close to the border were able to pick up CBC radio and television. They liked what they saw and heard and wanted something similar. We forget too that much of the best programming on PBS is British and Canadian, and that only one to two per cent of the American public watches PBS. And we forget that PBS's more and more frequent pleas for money are at least as annoying as commercials.

How did we get to the present situation anyway? By the late 1920s, eighty per cent of the radio programmes Canadians listened to were American. Canadians preferred the slicker American product. Part of the problem was that Canadians even had trouble receiving Canadian stations because of the interference of far more powerful American stations. The Liberal government of Mackenzie King was urged to do something, and in 1928 it established a royal commission under the chairmanship of Sir John Aird, a banker. Aird, it seems safe to assume, was not overly sympathetic to the intrusion of the state in matters of private enterprise. Nonetheless, in 1929, the Aird Commission recommended the creation of a public body to regulate the private stations and to broadcast programmes of its own. The commission also urged the creation of Canadian networks. (In 1929, stations in Toronto and Montreal had become affiliates of American networks. And the Aird Commission had learned in New York that NBC was planning to expand its system to cover the whole of North America.)

In 1932, at the height of the Depression, the Conservative government of R.B. Bennett announced the establishment of the Canadian Radio Broadcasting Commission (CRBC). "This country," said Bennett during the debate that resulted in the founding of the CRBC, "must be assured of complete Canadian control of broadcasting from Canadian sources free from foreign interference or influence. Without such control, radio broadcasting can never become a great agency for the communication of matters of national concern and for the diffusion of national thought and ideals, and without such control it can never be the agency by which national consciousness may be fostered and sustained, and national unity still further strengthened." The CRBC came on the air in 1933. Regrettably, it was underfunded from the beginning. (Underfunding, one could argue, has been a continuing problem of Canadian public broadcasting.) At the end of its life in 1936, the CRBC owned only three stations and leased four others. Its six hours a day of programming reached less than half of Canada's population.

In 1936, the Liberal government of Mackenzie King disbanded the CRBC and created the CBC. "To the CBC," writes Bruce Raymond, "fell the task of linking together a country larger than the United States with the resources of a population scarcely larger than that of New York City." Like the CRBC, the CBC was *a single system*; it not only provided public broadcasting, it also regulated private broadcasters. The job of the CBC was to keep all of Canadian broadcasting in perspective. But the central element was the public component. Funding for the CBC during these years came from three sources: commercials, radio licences (the fee remained $2.50 a year until 1953, when licences were abolished) and the federal treasury. By the time the CBC was ten years old it had extended its reach to ninety per cent of the population and was broadcasting eighteen hours a day.

But it took more than ten years for CBC radio to become

wholly and distinctively Canadian. In the early years, for example, the CBC imported a great many commercially-sponsored comedy programmes from the U.S. — *The Jell-O Programme* with Jack Benny, *The Chase and Sanborn Programme* with Edgar Bergen and Charlie McCarthy. Then came Canadian shows — *Woodhouse and Hawkins*, *The Allan Young Show* and *Wayne and Shuster* — shows in the American mould. Only later did such programmes as *Rawhide, Funny You Should Say That, Inside From the Outside, The Royal Canadian Air Farce, Dr. Bundolo* and *The Frantics* come along — programmes that were more British than American and more Canadian than either.

Look at drama. In the early years, when the CBC wasn't actually broadcasting American dramatic shows, it was using American scripts. The Americans seemed to have warehouses full of them, and they were cheap. It took a while for the CBC to discover that Canadian scripts that told good Canadian stories were better. In 1944, eight years after the CBC began, the *Stage* series was born and quickly became the finest radio drama programme on the continent. During this period, every region developed its own distinctive dramatic shows. *Youngbloods of Beaver Bend*, for example, originated in Winnipeg.

During the Second World War, the CBC finally established its own news service. Until then, it had used the wire services. We got our own propaganda shows too: *Theatre of Freedom, L is for Lanky, Soldier's Wife*. After the war came the magazine shows — *Assignment, Project* and, best of all, *CBC Wednesday Night*, an unabashedly high-brow programme launched in 1947. By the mid-1950s, twenty years after its birth, the only American programme left on CBC radio was the Metropolitan Opera broadcast. The rest of the schedule had been Canadianized. The trouble was that not too many of us were listening to Canadian radio any more. Or to American radio. We were watching television. American television. In more recent years, the novelty of television has worn off. A lot of us are listening to radio again. And we've come to celebrate the existence and distinctiveness of CBC radio.

II

Canadianizing CBC television has been a much slower and more difficult process than Canadianizing CBC radio.

In 1949 Parliament authorized the CBC to move into television production. Two years later the Royal Commission on National Development in the Arts, Letters and Sciences (The Massey Report) reaffirmed the role of public broadcasting in Canada. The CBC, it said, had developed "into the greatest single agency for national unity, understanding, and enlightenment. Despite inevitable limitations it has exceeded all reasonable expectations....The CBC is in general performing its duty satisfactorily, even admirably, in providing appropriate and varied programmes." According to Massey, public broadcasting had three objectives: to provide "adequate coverage of the entire population," to provide "opportunities for Canadian talent, and for Canadian self-expression," and, most importantly, to offer *"successful resistance to the absorption of Canada into the general cultural pattern of the United States."* [My emphasis.] Despite a concerted effort by private broadcasters to persuade the Massey Commission that an independent regulatory agency for broadcasting should be established, the commission recommended the continuation of a single system presided over by the CBC. The Massey Report argued prophetically that "a completely separate body treating public and private radio broadcasting with judicial impartiality could not fail to destroy the present system upon which we depend for national coverage with national programmes." In 1955 Robert

Fowler, head of a royal commission into broadcasting, again recommended the retention of the single system. As well, he proposed the establishment of a fixed funding formula for the CBC, funding that would not be at the whim of Parliament. (Although that proposal has been made repeatedly in the years since, it has never been adopted.)

Pressure by the private broadcasters continued, and in 1958 the Conservative government of John Diefenbaker put an end to the single system, which had been in effect since 1932. The Broadcasting Act of 1958 established a separate regulatory body, the Board of Broadcast Governors. The BBG was to be responsible for overseeing the relationship between Canada's public and private broadcasters, as well as "ensuring the continued existence and efficient operation of a national broadcasting system" — the CBC. One of the BBG's early acts was a decision to grant permission to private television broadcasters to establish their own network. CTV came on air in 1961. From the beginning, as I've already indicated, it relied almost entirely on American and American-style entertainment programming. Only its news, current affairs and sports programming were largely Canadian.

In 1965 Robert Fowler was again invited by the Liberals to examine Canadian broadcasting. He blamed its growing problems on a Parliament and a government that hadn't clearly defined what it wanted broadcasting to achieve. A year later, a Liberal White Paper on broadcasting stated that "the place of the public element should predominate in policy areas where a choice between the two is involved." It too recommended a fixed funding formula for the CBC on a per capita basis. But despite higher distribution costs than any broadcasting system in the world (plus the need to produce programming in two languages), the CBC has continued to receive far less money per capita than public broadcasting systems elsewhere. (With half the staff, the CBC produces twice as much programming as the BBC.)

The Broadcasting Act of 1968, brought in by the Trudeau Liberals, replaced the BBG with the Canadian Radio Television Commission (CRTC). On one point at least the new Broadcasting Act echoed the White Paper of 1966. Section 3(h) states: *"Where any conflict arises between the objectives of the national broadcasting service and the interests of the private element of the Canadian broadcasting system, it shall be resolved in the public interest, but paramount consideration shall be given to the objectives of the national broadcasting service."* [My emphasis.] In other words, the CBC is the heart, the centrepiece of the Canadian broadcasting system. Everything else takes second place.

When Canadian — CBC — television began in 1952, Torontonians had already been watching American television from Buffalo for four years. (In those days, incredible as it now seems, Torontonians who wanted a night on the town used to drive the ninety miles to Buffalo. American TV, as critic Bob Blackburn once put it, meant Torontonians could stay at home and still go to Buffalo.) In the years since 1952, although the number of Canadian stations available to Canadians has grown more rapidly than the number of American stations, the viewing pattern established in television's early years hasn't changed. Torontonians spend most of their viewing time watching American television, much of it on Canadian channels. The following list shows the channels I receive in my east-end Toronto home. I subscribe to Rogers Cable television, rent a converter and subscribe as well to a package of seven Pay-TV channels, almost all of whose material is American.

Channel

2 Ontario's publicly-owned educational channel, OECA

3 Global, a privately-owned network based in Ontario

4 MTV, a privately-owned multi-lingual, multi-cultural channel

5 WBEN, CBS's Buffalo affiliate (see also Ch. 16)

6 CBLT, CBC's Toronto English-language outlet

7 CITY TV, a privately-owned Toronto channel

8 CFTO, flagship station of CTV, a privately-owned national network

9 WKBW, ABC's Buffalo affiliate (see also Ch. 17)

10 Rogers Cable community channel

11 CHCH, Hamilton, a privately-owned channel

12 CBLFT, Toronto's CBC French-language outlet

13 WGRZ, NBC's Buffalo affiliate

14 Pay-TV preview channel/Parliament

15 CKVR, CBC's Barrie affiliate

16 WBEN, CBS's Buffalo affiliate (see also Ch. 5)

17 WKBW, ABC's Buffalo affiliate (see also Ch. 9)

18 CHEX, CBC's Peterborough affiliate

19 CKCO, CTV's Kitchener affiliate

20 WNED, PBS's Buffalo affiliate

21 WUTV, independent Rochester channel

22 TV Guide

23 Arts and Entertainment Network (Pay-TV)

24 First Choice/Superchannel Movies (Pay-TV)

25 Cable Network News (Pay-TV)

26 Sports Network (Pay-TV)

27 Nashville Network (Pay-TV)

28 Learning Channel (Pay-TV)

29 MuchMusic (Pay-TV)

31 Premier Choix (Pay-TV)

32 Chinavision

33 Rebroadcast of MTV programmes

Canadians who live outside Toronto have never had much love for the place, but they insist on their inalienable right to have what Torontonians have. If Torontonians can get the three commercial American networks CBS, NBC and ABC, plus PBS, everybody in Canada should be able to get three commercial American networks plus PBS. That this may not be in the interests of Canadian broadcasting is beside the point. Equally beside the point is that it's a simple accident of geography that Toronto gets those channels. (Toronto is, after all, right across the lake from Buffalo.) In the years before 1968, it was possible for the Board of Broadcast Governors, and after 1968, for the CRTC, to tell a viewer in Edmonton, for example, "Sorry, but we just can't give you four American channels. You live too far away from the border. You'll have to make do with the American programming you get on Canadian stations."

Cable changed that. Cable made it possible for most Canadians to get two, three, four and more American channels. In a sense, cable and the CRTC moved the American border two hundred miles north. (Everyone now lived across the lake from Buffalo.) That's why Canada is the most cabled country in the world — not just because cable provides a clearer image (which it does) but because it provides ready access to more American television. The result, of course, has been the further fragmentation of the viewing audience. The more stations there are, the fewer people watch any given station.

The Broadcasting Act of 1968 included a provision,

added almost as an afterthought, giving the CRTC responsibility to oversee the integration of cable into the Canadian broadcasting system. According to Section 3(b) of the act, the Canadian broadcasting system "should be effectively owned and controlled by Canadians so as to safeguard, enrich, and strengthen the cultural, political, social, and economic fabric of Canada." The very next section of the Broadcasting Act, Section 3(c), states that "the right of persons to receive programmes...is unquestioned." In other words, the Canadian broadcasting system is supposed to strengthen Canadian society, but if Canadians want to see a lot of American programmes on cable, that's OK too. The most difficult and crucial task of the CRTC from its beginnings has been its attempt to reconcile Sections 3(b) and 3(c) of the act. I believe the CRTC has failed us badly in that attempt.

Through a series of unwise decisions, the CRTC has done much to undermine Canadian broadcasting. It has not, to repeat Massey, offered "successful resistance to the absorption of Canada into the general cultural pattern of the United States." Indeed, the CRTC has demonstrated itself to be a remarkably slow learner. In many ways, the CBC has never been better, but the context in which it exists has changed so much that it's not so much the heart of Canadian broadcasting as just another player. Despite Section 3(h), the CRTC has not given paramount consideration to the objectives of the CBC but rather has given more and more power to the private sector. Consider the following:

CABLE   The decision to allow cable television to remain in private hands was, I think, a serious mistake. If the CRTC had established a crown corporation for cable, with profits directed either to the CBC's programme budget or to a body such as Telefilm Canada, there would be far more genuinely Canadian programming on the air today.

(The cable industry's revenues — including Pay-TV — are now upwards of $1 billion a year.)

GLOBAL   The decision to establish a second private English-language network simply didn't make sense. The CRTC's experience with CTV should have taught the agency that it was unreasonable to expect private television to make a real contribution to Canadian entertainment programming. For one thing, Canadian entertainment programming is too expensive. It's from three to six times more costly to produce than news and game shows. In any case, why produce Canadian entertainment programmes that are certain to lose money when American programmes that are certain to make money can be acquired at ten per cent of the cost? And especially when one can easily get around the CRTC's Canadian content regulations. All Global could reasonably be expected to do was add to the growing homogeneity of the material available to us. The irony, as cultural critic Paul Audley has pointed out, is that the more stations there are in a market, the fewer real choices there are.

(It must be remembered that these first two decisions were taken under the chairmanship of Pierre Juneau. He established a pattern of CRTC decision-making that has succeeded over the years in undermining the central role of the CBC in the Canadian broadcasting system. That Juneau should now preside over a CBC he helped emasculate is an enormous irony. It seems astonishing in retrospect that Juneau's appointment wasn't given the kind of scrutiny it deserved from the Conservative opposition and the press. Juneau, after all, was a Liberal being appointed to a non-partisan post.)

PAY-TV   The decision to license competing Pay-TV services whose chief product was American film made even less sense than the decision to license a second English-language network. Everything that had been said on the subject in the years leading up to the decision led one to hope for more, especially in light of the following statements. John Roberts, Secretary of State (1975): "I am determined that pay-TV...not become a Trojan horse for still more cultural penetration." Harry Boyle, chairman of the CRTC (1976): "We consider the introduction of pay-television to be an important and serious first step towards the repossession of a Canadian broadcasting system." A CRTC position paper (1978): "We are determined that pay-television shall develop to primarily benefit Canadian broadcasting, the programme production industry, and Canadian creative talent." As late as 1982, the CRTC stated that it had "found persuasive the arguments presented at the hearing that a desirable way of ensuring the evolution of a distinctively Canadian pay-television system may well be through the adoption of a universal pay-television service."

Nonetheless, as Paul Audley writes, "In the face of the advice of virtually all applicants and intervenors, and despite analysis carried out by its own staff...the CRTC proceeded to do precisely what it had said it would not do. Rather than licensing a number of complementary services, which most applicants and intervenors had favoured, the commission licensed directly competing commercial services based on Hollywood feature films." We all know the result. In the summer of 1984, First Choice and Superchannel merged to form, in effect, a monopoly. Within months, the two companies were urging the CRTC to ease their Canadian content quotas. (Thirty per cent of the air time on Pay-TV must be devoted to Canadian material.) But Canadian content on Pay-TV has already been very loosely defined. It has included the Toronto taping of the New York musical *Something's Afoot*; Canadian-taped specials starring George Burns, Crystal

Gayle and Red Skelton; soft-core porn soap operas — *Loving Friends and Perfect Couples*, for example, in which Canadian actors play secondary roles; and films such as *A Case of Libel* starring Ed Asner and *Nobody Makes Me Cry* with Elizabeth Taylor and Carol Burnett. Canadian films tend to be the atrociously dubbed ones I mentioned earlier, and the odd quality film (*J.A. Martin, photographe*) screened at 7 a.m. Genuine, fresh, Canadian content has consisted of the movies *The Wild Pony*, *Quebec/Canada 1995* and *The Terry Fox Story*; a TV version of Mavis Gallant's *What Is to be Done?*; Linda Griffiths in *Maggie and Pierre*; and specials with Bruce Cockburn and Howie Mandel.

First Choice made no secret of the fact that the only kind of Canadian programmes it could produce to meet its obligations to investors were programmes that would be acceptable in the international market. But as Patrick Watson has said, "That can only mean co-production with U.S. (and British and maybe French) interests, and it is not hard to guess...who will have to yield on matters of taste and content and cultural orientation."

CBC 2   The decision to deny CBC 2 was foolish. In an attempt to respond to the changed environment in which it found itself, the CBC requested permission from the CRTC to launch a second network on cable. CBC 2 — a kind of TV equivalent of FM radio — would rebroadcast some programmes from CBC 1, like *The National*, but it would also provide new programmes for minority tastes. The request was denied. The CRTC felt the $30 million cost was too high and that the audience on cable would be too limited.

SUPERSTATIONS   Equally foolish was the decision to permit superstations. Privately-owned TV stations in Hamilton, Edmonton, Vancouver and Montreal requested the

CRTC's permission to be seen in medium-sized cities across Canada. (Their signal would be delivered by satellite to local cable companies.) The idea was to increase TV viewing options in underserved communities. The CRTC granted the request, arguing that the superstations would contribute to "the critical struggle for a distinctive and strong Canadian broadcasting system." How they would do that given the amount of American programming they carry wasn't made clear. What was clear was that the CRTC had become a master of Doublespeak.

We've seen in this chapter how the need for the CBC arose and how a Conservative government responded. We've seen, too, how the context in which the CBC exists has changed since cable came on the scene. Government's response to the changed environment has been the establishment of a number of committees and task forces to study the situation. Dozens of position papers have been published. But except for the Broadcast Development Fund, little has been done. Meanwhile, the place of the CBC in our cultural life has been permitted to erode. In the absence of a clear direction from Parliament, the CRTC has attempted to fill the policy vacuum. It has failed. The next chapter deals with some of the implications of the increasingly homogeneous television environment that surrounds us.

Implications

I

Little is known for certain about the physiology of watching television — exactly what the brain does to and with the material our eyes take in from the TV screen. All one can do is make educated guesses. The model of how the brain works that makes most sense to me is that set forth by Paul MacLean, head of the Laboratory for Brain Evolution and Behavior at the National Institute for Mental Health in Washington. His view has been elaborated on by Arthur Koestler, among others.

According to the MacLean model, the brain consists of essentially two parts — the neocortex (new brain) and the paleocortex (old brain). The neocortex, the outer layer, is the newest and most highly developed part of the brain. It is the seat of logic and verbal language; it's the centre of our rational faculties and of voluntary behaviour.

The older and relatively primitive paleocortex, which occupies the large central portion of the brain, has been inherited from our reptilian and mammalian past. ("Speaking allegorically," says MacLean, "when the psychiatrist bids a patient to lie on the couch, he is asking him to stretch out alongside a horse and a crocodile.") The paleocortex is compulsive, ritualistic, addicted to precedent. It's the seat of our feelings, our passions and what Jung called our "collective unconscious." Our understanding of symbolic (non-verbal) language is centred in the paleocortex, which functions viscerally. It controls our autonomic nervous system — those parts of the body (the glands, for example) that are not usually subject to conscious control.

Central to the paleocortex or old brain is the hippocampus; it collects all our sensations and relays bits and pieces of this information to other parts of the brain. The hippocampus appears to affect all brain activity; it can excite or inhibit our thinking or our emotions. The hippocampus is especially responsive to the content of high jpm television. It "likes" loud sounds, things that move a lot, sexual explicitness and innuendo, physical and verbal acts of aggression. That's the kind of language the old brain not only understands but thrives on — the language of the hunt. That language gets our juices flowing and rewards us with pleasurable feelings. But while that's happening, the higher functions of the brain, those located in the neocortex and involved in cognitive functions — analysis and judgment — are turned off. Which helps explain the mindless, passive appearance we often have when sitting in front of a television set (or a fireplace, for that matter).

The fact is that we are dealing here with a reward system that is irrational, that is not in our best interests as human beings. As Aldous Huxley suggested, our glandular system, which is "admirably well adapted to life in paleolithic times," is not at all well suited to life now. We produce far more adrenalin than is good for us. Arthur Koestler's view is even more gloomy. He believed that the human brain suffered from an evolutionary "design error," a split between our thought and our feelings, between the human and the animal in us that couldn't be bridged. The only solution, he felt, was biochemical intervention, a kind of physiological censorship. In Norman Jewison's film *Rollerball*, the only outlet for aggression permitted by rulers is rollerball, a savage game which combines the most violent elements of hockey, roller derby, motorcycle racing and the martial arts.

Not only is it possible to become addicted to high jpm television, but many of us do. The amount of time the average person spends watching TV continues to increase. In the U.S. it's thirty hours a week or about an hour more per day than in Canada. The process, I suspect, is not unlike that which occurs when rats who've had electrodes implanted in the pleasure centres of their brains continue to stimulate themselves even at the expense of doing their bodies harm — starving, for example. (In his novel *Mind Killer*, Spider Robinson projects us into a future world in which people "give themselves over to the ultimate addiction: they stimulate their cerebral pleasure centres directly with pulses of electric current." In David Cronenberg's *Videodrome*, a futurist film about our insatiable appetite for ever more jolts from television, poor people — those who have no TV sets — go to a Cathode Ray Mission. They go not to eat, as poor people of an earlier time might, but to spend time in a private booth with a television set, absorbing their daily doses of high jpm television.)

There are groups — the National Coalition on Television Violence in the U.S., for example — who are convinced that anyone who watches ten to fifteen hours of high jpm television a week "is unconsciously affected in a harmful way. The most common effects are significant increases in anger and irritability and a desensitization towards violence." (The networks, of course, reject this conclusion; they've done research that proves the contrary.) According to George Gerbner, TV causes those who watch more than four hours a day to find the world more dangerous than those who watch it two hours or less.

Michelle Landsberg writes, echoing Neil Postman's *The*

Disappearance of Childhood, "One of the most devastating charges that future generations will be able to hurl against the TV merchandisers is that they stole away the child's birthright of play. Teachers report that children have lost not only the knowledge of the old games — the rhymes, chants and rules — but even the imaginative power to invent new ones. Parents say that when they limit their children's TV-watching to a well-chosen half-hour each day, the youngsters' resilience, energy, good humour, and playfulness come surging back."

II

Until the middle of the twentieth century boredom remained a largely upper-middle-class affliction. No other class had leisure time enough not only to be bored, but to realize it was bored. The eight-hour day and television arrived on the scene at approximately the same time — just after the Second World War. The eight-hour day democratized boredom. Now we all had enough time to be bored. And we turned to television to while away some of our new-found hours of quiet desperation. The trouble is that television may be at least as dehumanizing as ten-and-twelve-hour working days used to be.

Our daily lives, it seems to me, come more and more to resemble high jpm television. There is an increasingly rapid turnover in our relationships and pursuits. If marriages on soap operas now last an average of only eighteen months, those on this side of the screen appear to be catching up quickly. Many of us are into photography one month and yoga the next. Our boredom thresholds are such that we can't stick with anybody or anything for very long. "Doesn't anyone stay in one place any more?" sings Carole King. "Like I was into ecology," says a hitchhiker in *Blue Highways — A Journey Into America*, "but it got boring." Can anyone imagine Einstein saying that about physics? It's unclear whether the rapid turnover in our relationships and pursuits is good for us; but there's no doubt that it's good for the economy. We want to look nice and smell nice for our new lovers. Each new hobby has its own accoutrements that one shouldn't be without.

I wonder about the implications for democracy of the increasingly high jpm world we live in. One of the tests of democracy, after all, is the capacity of ordinary people to endure boredom — the boredom of reading tedious reports and attending seemingly endless meetings. There's no doubt that the more complex society becomes the more a capacity to endure that kind of boredom is required. In fact, we have less. The only thing we seem to have the patience to change is our own lifestyles, and that we seem to do endlessly. Certainly it's a marvellous irony that at the very moment we've lost whatever patience we might have had for observing Parliamentary debate, proceedings of the House of Commons become available to us on television.

Boredom has affected politics in other ways. Charles Citrine is onto something, I suspect, when he argues in *Humboldt's Gift* that boredom, not justice, may be what some modern political revolutions are about. Boredom, says Norman Podhoretz, echoing Citrine, "is the most underrated force in human affairs." And it's interesting to observe the ways in which radical politics have changed in the last quarter century. It used to be that if you were a radical, you devoted your whole life to your radical cause. One thinks of Gandhi or Martin Luther King or J.S. Woodsworth. But some American radicals who've grown up in the age of television are different. They often do a stint in support of one radical cause and then move on to something radically different. In the 1960s Jerry Rubin led an American revolutionary movement, the Yippies; in the 1980s he's a Wall Street broker who, among other things, runs a singles bar and is an apologist for the Yuppies. In the 1960s Eldridge Cleaver led the Black Panthers; today he's a born-again Christian and a supporter of Ronald Reagan.

Mainstream politics have been affected too. Public opinion fluctuates so wildly that it's become increasingly difficult for pollsters to make predictions with any accuracy. "The swings and yaws," writes Dalton Camp, "are now so commonplace that any politician imprudent enough to crow about a favourable poll today is almost certain to be eating crow tomorrow." One day we're told that the federal Liberals under John Turner have an insurmountable lead over the Conservatives. The next day those predictions are proved wrong.

And we know about looks. The trouble with Joe Clark, poor bugger, is that he looks Canadian. So does Robert Stanfield. They have too few jpm's. Pierre Trudeau and Brian Mulroney, on the other hand, look as if they could be leaders not just of a country like Canada, but of *real* countries like France or the U.S. To be effective on television not only must you look a certain way, but you have to talk a certain way as well. The press made fun of Jesse Jackson's penchant for using catch phrases and slogans in his campaign for the American presidency. But as Jackson explained, "Sometimes when we speak grammatically that's not enough...we have to speak epigrammatically... because when you grow up in the mass media era, when you have these fifteen- and thirty-second bites, you must be able to use the language so you can get out a significant message in a very short space of time." And it worked. Jackson got and continues to get a lot of attention.

III

Video games and rock videos are the ultimate in high jpm television. There are now video games to suit every taste, almost all of them of a kill or be killed nature. If you're "into" science, there's a video game called "Evolution" that requires you to pass through six stages of development from amoeba to human while avoiding electronic extinction. When you reach the human stage, stage six, you're "rewarded" by being destroyed in a nuclear war; you return to being an amoeba, and start all over again. Each time through the game, the destructive forces are faster and more unpredictable. The game has ninety-nine levels of difficulty. Even the game's creators have only evolved to level forty.

If you're into Jesus, there's a video car race for you. The game asks the question, "Do you know that Jesus is the way?" You have to keep a speeding car on the twisting roadway of life. To go off the road is to fall into sin. But maybe you would like to fall into sin? There's a video game called "Hold Up." If you kill the bank tellers before they trip their alarm, you win. Another game called "Lover Boy" awards points for the "successful rape" of four naked women chased through a maze. In "Dragon's Lair" the player becomes a barbarian who controls the violent animated action on the screen.

Video games are a cause of concern everywhere. In the Philippines, that friend of the democratic process, Ferdinand Marcos, outlawed video games in response to a public outcry. Filipinos believed the machines were "devilish" contraptions wreaking havoc on the morals of the young. And in the U.S. a total of $5 billion was spent on video games in 1982, twice as much as was spent going to the movies.

No wonder movies are becoming more and more fast-paced. "It's bam bam pow," writes Pauline Kael of George Lucas, the director of the *Star Wars* trilogy. But her words could equally apply to any one of a number of other directors. "He's like a slugger in the ring who has no variety and never lets up," she continues. "His movies are made on the assumption that the audience must be distracted every minute." "Visual rock 'n' roll" is the term George Miller, director of the cult film *Road Warrior*, uses to describe this approach to filmmaking. Young people have become so conditioned to fast-paced material, says Miller, that they can look at "video cassettes with the fast-forward button on. They're watching movies at maybe two or three times normal speed and still picking up enough information to follow the story."

Douglas Trumbull, who worked on special effects for George Lucas, has himself directed such high jpm films as *Brainstorm*. But Trumbull has wearied of traditional filmmaking; he's looking for new ways to intensify the film-viewing experience. He's developed a process for projecting films at sixty frames per second rather than at the present twenty-four. Viewers respond (as measured physiologically) at a rate *five times* faster than their response when the same material is projected at twenty-four frames. The experience is so intense that viewers estimate the length of a ten-minute film as being considerably longer. Trumbull predicts the development of "the microfeature, a high-impact sensory experience, compressed in time."

Isn't that what a rock video is, a kind of ultra high jpm microfeature whose visuals frequently have nothing to do with the music and seem thrown in for shock value? It's not surprising to discover that many successful filmmakers — Tobe Hooper of *The Texas Chainsaw Massacre* and William Friedkin, for example — are now directing rock videos, and that rock video directors are being invited to make feature films.

Advertisers are moving to the fifteen-second commercial. Just over ten years ago the sixty-second spot was the standard length; thirty-second spots were regarded as unacceptable. Les Brown of *Channels of Communication* magazine doesn't rule out "the possibility of the radically speeded-up five-second spot...that would get to you almost on the subliminal level." Ad agencies such as Vision Systems want to go even further. They want to display product information on video screens in stores and windows. Vision Systems has developed Videofile, a giant screen — two and a half feet by five feet — which, combined with a repeating video cassette recorder, presents advertising designed "to stop people in their tracks." In Al Razutis's experimental film *America*, billboards have all become huge video screens. In the city of the future in *Blade Runner*, the Goodyear blimp becomes a huge floating video screen at night.

Not just film and television are speeding up. Serious books and magazines have more and more difficulty getting published. In order to survive, *Harper's* has become a kind of intellectual *Reader's Digest*.* Bookstore shelves are increasingly filled with non-books — books for people who really don't like reading: self-help guides, books by and about celebrities, thrillers, instant books — books, as American writer William Gass puts it, that stand to literature as fast food does to eating. A lot of writers, says Gass, "are writing for the fast mind that speeds over the text like those noisy bastards in motorboats." I know good writers who have been rejected by publishers on the

---

* Some years ago *TV Guide* asked me to write an article outlining my jpm theory. I did so in the style you've been reading in this book. *TV Guide*'s editor thought my prose much too slow for his readers. He rewrote the piece. The revised version began, "Every September, the three U.S. television networks sit down to their high stakes poker game." I asked to have my name taken off the published piece.

grounds that they write prose that requires concentration; one was told that it's impossible to read him and watch TV at the same time.

Marshall McLuhan argued that people had stopped reading books in the early-to-mid-1960s. They'd begun to sample them instead. "The unread book," he said, "is the normal thing of our world.... I have only a few minutes in which to look at any of the books I have around here. I have to sample quickly and take them back to the library. Every day five or six new books come in that I can only sample, I can't read. But that's normal. The book is no longer something for reading." Pay-TV now allows me to sample current movies the same way.

Professional sports have also been affected by television. Hockey, for instance, has become a much higher scoring game emphasizing offense at the expense of defense. Former NHL player Eric Nesterenko wrote after seeing a game in which Toronto beat Chicago 10-8: "I cannot remember...a game in which 18 goals were scored. The single attribute that makes the pro game different from the amateur is the quality of the defensive play. It is the part that gives a game its pace, tension, flow, and makes the especially well-executed score so exciting and so meaningful. In *good* hockey, most scoring plays fail;...18 goals are boring. They indicate terribly ragged play. There is no premium on skill." But in sports, as in all television, unsubtle drives out subtle. Veteran football player Charlie Joiner makes a similar point. "When I started [in the late 1960s]," he says, "quarterbacks averaged about eighteen passes a game. Now it's more than thirty." The reason, he says, is television.

IV

So what's to be done? Nothing, says Jerry Mander in *Four Arguments for the Elimination of Television*; the medium of television can no more be reformed than can guns. The only real solution, Mander believes, is the total abolition of TV. Otherwise we're doomed. Well, obviously that's not going to happen.

Censorship isn't the answer either, although even the BBC has tried it. (It banned the Rolling Stones' video *Under Cover of the Night* because of its images of blood, torture and violent death in Central America.) Certainly, none of what I've said to this point should be read as an argument for censorship. As a member in good standing of the Canadian Civil Liberties Association, I am opposed to censorship of any kind. I believe it does more harm than good. But that's not to say I think TV has no effect. I'm sure it does — for good and for ill. In 1980, for example, during the week after the Fonz took out a library card on an episode of *Happy Days*, the number of young people applying for membership in libraries across the U.S. increased by five *hundred* per cent. Surely that's no coincidence. It seems safe to assume that the Fonz's behaviour caused the increase. Television undoubtedly causes other things too. There are numerous cases on record of people who have seen a crime committed on TV and who have gone out and committed the same crime. Rowell Huesmann, a psychology professor at the University of Illinois, has been following 800 viewers since they were in grade three. It appears, says Huesmann, that "high television viewers and high violence viewers are more likely to be convicted of more serious crimes." "If you believe," Irving Kristol wrote long before he became a famous neoconservative, "that no one was ever corrupted by a book, you have also to believe that no one was ever improved by a book (or a play or a movie). You have to believe, in other words, that all art is morally trivial."

According to a soon to be published study, *The Impact of Television: A Natural Experiment Involving Three Communities*, children's sex role attitudes become more strongly stereotyped in the presence of TV. That's no surprise given that men still out-number women 3:1 on American TV. (The men tend to be fifty-five or younger, the women thirty-five or younger.) Although I haven't seen any figures, I have no doubt that CBC television is far less sexually stereotyped. It's less stereotyped in its treatment of old people too.

A character in David Cronenberg's *Videodrome* says at one point, "The battle for the mind will be fought in the video arena." Will be? The battle for the mind *is* being fought in the video arena. And the mind is losing. Television has become Aldous Huxley's soma, only it's ingested visually instead of orally. And Huxley, not Orwell, it turns out, was right. Big Brother isn't watching us. It's far more subtle than that. We're watching Big Brother.

And we have only seen the beginning. Audio-Visual Reinforcement Techniques Inc. is an American company that produces audiotapes and videotapes containing subliminal messages. Videotapes used at staff training sessions subliminally "instill loyalty, encourage diligence, and reduce absenteeism." Audiotapes heard in supermarkets and department stores tell us, "You are honest. You won't steal. You will be caught if you do, and you will go to jail." The possibility exists that these techniques can and will be used on television.

So what's to be done?

Conclusions

"Act locally; think globally." — Jacques Ellul

I

The title of Hilda Neatby's 1953 critical study of Canadian education, *So Little for the Mind*, also applies to much of what's on television. But the fact is that there *is* more for the mind on CBC television than on all of Canadian and American private television put together. And, despite Jerry Mander, I believe that there are choices. They may not be as dramatic as abolishing television, or censoring it, but they're real nonetheless.

There's no doubt that CBC television is a countervailing force against the homogeneity of American commercial television and its Canadian imitators. It's different in structure; it's different in mood and tone. We've come to realize that CBC radio is not just a convenience, it's a necessity. The same thing is true of CBC television. Everything possible therefore must be done politically and economically to assure a strong continuing role for the CBC. Politically, we as citizens and viewers have to care enough to put pressure on a Parliament which has strong doubts about whether the CBC really matters to us. Then we need an all-party agreement not only on the fundamental importance of the CBC but on a long-term funding formula on a per-capita basis that assures both the corporation's financial independence and the kind of arm's-length relationship from government that it needs.

(There have been too many examples of government interference in the affairs of the CBC, none more blatant than during the imposition of the War Measures Act in 1970. Gérard Pelletier, secretary of state in 1970, phoned several important media figures, including George Davidson, then president of the CBC. He later said he called Davidson as an "individual" rather than as the minister to whom Davidson was responsible. Davidson, on the other hand, was sure Pelletier was acting as an official government spokesman. But he insisted Pelletier's call hadn't influenced him. Whatever the truth, it's clear that *after* their conversation the CBC began censoring itself in what became the most shameful episode in its history. On October 15, a day *before* the War Meaures Act was brought in, Peter Trueman, then executive producer of CBC's national news, was called into his superior's office. In his book *Smoke & Mirrors* Trueman recalls: "We were to avoid commentary and speculation of all kinds. We were not to use man-on-the-street interviews or shoot film of any public demonstration. We were to air no panel discussions on the October Crisis and were to avoid reporting speculation, particularly speculation about what the government was doing." The irony is that the CBC couldn't even get its censorship act together. The night Pierre Laporte's body was found, the CBC continued to broadcast the one thing it *should* have kept quiet about. It was still announcing that the body of James Cross had also been found, long after the news had been officially denied.)

How much the CBC will cost taxpayers is difficult to know. Certainly it will be more than it is now. The Mulroney Conservatives' decision to cut $75 million from the CBC's budget succeeded only in further undermining the already low morale at the corporation. Because the truth is, as Carleton professor Bruce Doern writes in *How Ottawa Spends*, the CBC is "overmandated and underfinanced."

We may be talking about $1.25 billion a year, or about one and a half times the CBC's present budget. (I'm not including the revenue from commercials in these figures.) That means $50 a year for every Canadian.

That's a lot of money. But let's put that amount into perspective. The budget for Canada's military defence is more than $10 billion a year. And we're told that's not enough. Jean-Jacques Blais, our former defence minister, has said that our armed forces are seriously under-manned and underequipped. We're "overly vulnerable to enemy attack," he believes. But one could argue that on the cultural front we're not just vulnerable to attack, we're under attack. Every hour of every day. Do we believe in cultural defence? And if so, how much is our cultural defence worth? Our new minister of defence wants to improve our military defences by building six new frigates at a cost of $3 billion — or $500,000,000 per frigate. Is the CBC, the bulwark of our cultural defence, worth two and a half frigates a year?

At the same time that we're giving the CBC the money it needs to do the job only it can do, we have to be more realistic about the rest of Canadian television. The CRTC (and Parliament), as I argued earlier, have failed us. We can't return to a time when Canadians spent fifty percent of their time watching *Canadian* television. We may have to accept twenty-five percent. It's too late to nationalize cable. It seems impossible to formulate Canadian content rules that work. Maybe we should just forget about trying to Canadianize CTV, Global, Superchannel *et al.* Why not let the private broadcasters show as much American programming, real and imitation, as they like. But since it's a very profitable business, let's place a tax on their import of foreign programmes and films. Or a surtax on their considerable profits — the money to be used to reduce the taxpayers' bill. Similarly, let's place a surtax on cable profits. Then let's direct all our attention to something we not only can but must do something about — improving the CBC.

II

In keeping with a clearly defined role, and increased funding, CBC English-language television has to be better, much better, than it now is. That it's already better than it's ever been isn't good enough; the context in which the CBC exists has changed too much for that to be acceptable. Here are some of the things that need to improve. (I'm much less familiar with the French network and won't presume to suggest what should happen there.)

- We need a second CBC network (CBC 2), a TV equivalent of FM radio. Part of what makes CBC radio so good is that there are two networks and have been for years. CBC 2 would rebroadcast some programmes from CBC 1 — *The National, The Journal, the fifth estate, Charlie Grant's War.* But mostly it would also provide programmes for minority tastes. I, for one, miss good talk on TV, the kind that used to be the staple of such programmes as *The Watson Report*, a half-hour conversation between Patrick Watson and a guest. (*Joyce Davidson* on CTV was also good.) Talking heads no longer have mass appeal although there's still lots of good talk on Radio Canada. CBC 2 could provide such programming, conversations with some of our leading writers, artists, academics, politicians. CBC 2 would also inexpensively collect and show videotapes of live theatre, and dance and music from across the country. It would provide culture for people who don't live in metropolises and for the rest of us, a sense of what's happening in other regions. It could introduce a larger audience to video and performance art. Pilots of new shows might be tested on CBC 2.

- CBC television should get out of some areas of commercial broadcasting. There's little doubt that commercials trivialize dramatic shows and films.* Jean Pierre Lefebvre's *Les fleurs sauvages* was recently ruined by the English-language network. Not only was it cut up by commercials, but it was also dubbed. Surely discretion needs to be used. Single items on *The Journal* or *the fifth estate* are best left uncut. But I don't mind commercials between items on those shows. And certainly I don't mind commercials between shows. As well, the CBC's commercial acceptance policies need to be looked at. There are curious inconsistencies. It makes no sense to me to accept commercials for Pay-TV but to refuse those for private radio stations.

- CBC television should not repeat American programmes available elsewhere on the dial, *Dallas* and *Too Close for Comfort*, for example. We should, however, be able to see examples of programming from other countries around the world. *Worldwide*, for a time, was a show that gave us access to first-rate documentaries from other countries. Unfortunately, it was cancelled. (Meanwhile its French-language counterpart, *Télémonde*, is a big hit on Radio Canada.) *Worldwide*, its time and scope enlarged to include drama and other kinds of programming from around the world, should be returned to the schedule. If not the regular schedule, then CBC 2. And the CBC should stop being so reluctant in using subtitles. Subtitles, properly used, do work on television.

---

* We haven't had anything quite as tasteless happen at the CBC as occurred in Brazil when the series *Holocaust* was telecast. An insurance company ran commercials featuring Adolf Hitler. The company said Hitler was used "to show that you need life insurance, because you never know what's going to happen to you."

- The CBC should reverse its policy of shying away from airing controversial documentaries. It seems absurd that some NFB films, *Morgentaler*, for example, cannot be seen on the CBC simply because they have a point of view. Why not have a programme called *Point of View* that consists of the screening of controversial documentaries? Each episode might be followed by discussion and/or rebuttal.

- The CBC should by all means constantly evaluate its schedule and cancel programmes that are tired or weak. But shows shouldn't be cancelled simply because they've been on air for a long time. That appears to have been the sole reason for cancelling *The Friendly Giant*, as it was for cancelling *Chez Hélène* some years ago. I could much more readily understand the deletion of *Wayne and Shuster* from the schedule, a programme that used to be funny and no longer is.

- As someone with a particular interest in film history, I find it shameful that the English-language CBC hasn't followed the example of the French-language network in showing world film classics. On the French network one can regularly see first-rate prints of silent and sound film classics in clearly subtitled versions. The English network, on the other hand, almost always shows U.S. films. There's nothing wrong with yet another Paul Muni festival. But what about a Jean Gabin festival for a change? Or a French-Canadian film festival? The CBC could help ensure that adequately subtitled versions of the best French-Canadian films are available to English-Canadians. Filmmakers Gilles Carle and Jean-Pierre Lefebvre are virtually unknown in English Canada.

- There aren't enough reporters on *The National* covering the regions of Canada, let alone the regions of the world. The show is neither sufficiently national nor international. The CBC should have a permanent reporter in Africa and reporters in Central and South America. In the case of Africa and Latin America the CBC might consider sharing the work of the *Globe and Mail*'s excellent correspondents Michael Valpy and Oakland Ross. Elsewhere, the CBC would have to recruit and develop reporters of its own. That costs money. But it's not good enough simply to parachute a reporter into an area at a time of crisis — even if she's as good as Ann Medina.

- Most reporters on *The National* now shift so quickly from beat to beat that it's difficult to keep up, let alone have them build audience credibility. Just when I've come to trust Terry Milewski on science, he becomes a political reporter. Eve Savory seemed very good from the prairies. But now she's covering science. Give me more Mike Duffys — reporters who've spent half a lifetime covering an area. The CBC should do whatever is necessary to ensure that good reporters stick with their beats for as long as possible.

- There's a wealth of material in the CBC archives. *Rear View Mirror* on Sunday afternoons has been offering just a small sample of what's available. With the CBC's fiftieth anniversary coming up in 1986, I hope that programme is not only renewed but extended to run fifty-two weeks a year. And given a better time slot. Or maybe it should shown be in prime time on CBC 2.

- Arts coverage on CBC television needs to be improved. The reporting of arts events as news stories on *The National*, *The Journal* and *Midday* is obviously a step forward. But too often those reports tend to trivialize their subjects with their *People* magazine approach: here's W.P. Kinsella; he used to hustle pizza, now he hustles dreams. We need a CBC programme like radio's old *Critically Speaking*, a show on which intelligent, knowledgeable men and women talk about the arts. And particularly we need better criticism of CBC radio and television. Our newpapers and magazines don't do a good enough job and CBC programmers need to be kept on their toes.

- We need better media coverage on television, a programme that offers samples of editorial comment from print media across the country. That programme could also teach viewers about the media. It could show us how TV news is gathered and edited, and how that differs from what happens at a newspaper or at *Maclean's*. TV should do everything it can to demystify itself.

- We need a letters to the editor column — half an hour a day on CBC 2. Letters would be about any aspect of CBC programming and would be read by an announcer.

- In 1953 there were a total of 130 hours a year of in-house drama on the CBC English network. Today there are approximately seventy hours, or just over an hour a week. That includes everything — *The Beachcombers*, *Seeing Things*, *Charlie Grant's War*, etc. Obviously, that's not good enough. We need at least an hour a day or five times as much as we have now. There's no area of CBC television that needs expansion as much as drama. Canadians now spend fifty per cent of their viewing time watching popular drama. But only four per cent of the dramatic shows on TV are Canadian. According to the CRTC, "When news, public affairs and professional sports are removed, ninety percent of viewing is devoted to foreign produced entertainment programmes." In other words, we're importing our myths, dreams and fantasies.

- The CBC, and the provinces through their educational channels, have demonstrated that they can produce distinctive Canadian children's programmes. We need more of this kind of programming, especially from the CBC.

All of these things are going to cost money. Drama, in particular, is expensive, far more expensive to produce than information programming. I can think of no better fiftieth birthday present than a budget that finally allows the CBC to do what it's mandated to do. The CBC is writing the autobiography of Canada. It's important that it be well written.

III

There are two ways to combat the homogeneity of so much of what is on television. First, as I've already suggested, by providing more alternatives to the mind-numbing fare that dominates the airwaves. To that end a clearly defined, adequately funded and improved CBC will certainly make a difference. Secondly, we need to educate people — particularly young people — in how to watch television. Obviously, parents are an important influence. But it's also time we introduced television as a classroom subject. We've introduced sex education; more recently we've introduced the computer. Surely, television is at least as important a subject. Despite children's spending far more time watching television than they do anything other than sleeping, schools continue to pretend that TV doesn't exist. Like Michelle Landsberg, I too wonder when parents worry about strangers who might molest their children, whether they are equally "concerned about the molester who has possession of their child four hours a day."

One doesn't have to be a master pedagogue to come

up with useful classroom exercises. Even very young children can learn to watch TV more critically. Videotapes of commercials ("capitalist realism," as it was recently termed) can be screened and analyzed. How many times does the picture change in thirty seconds? Is that more often or less often than on other kinds of television programme? In addition to rapidly changing pictures, what else do commercials do to make us sit up and take notice? What kinds of roles do men and women have in commercials? How do TV commercials for toys and cereals get kids to go after their parents to buy those things? Young children can be encouraged to talk about and analyze their favourite and least favourite commmercials. They can try their hands at creating commercials.

Older children can begin to examine the structure of certain kinds of programme — the sitcom and the police show, for example. (After all, in English class they consider the structure of the ballad, yet they'll spend far more time watching sitcoms and police shows than they will reading ballads.) Then they can begin comparing particular sitcoms and police shows. What are the similarities and differences between *Newhart* and *Three's A Crowd*? Between *Cagney and Lacey* and *Miami Vice*? They can compare television news with newspaper news — what kind of news gets on TV and what kind doesn't. They can consider the treatment of women and children and old people on television. How realistic is the portrayal? Is that what old people they know are like? What differences are there between TV programmes produced in the U.S. and those in Canada? What, if anything, do those differences tell us about the two cultures?

I don't expect instant results. Obviously, it will take time. One has to remember that although everyone learns to read in school, there are still hundreds of thousands of illiterates and semi-literates among us. But I have no doubt that in the long run one of the results of a dispassionate look at television in our schools will be a greater appreciation of what the CBC does and still greater demands on it to serve us better.

When the CBC first came on the air in 1952, B.K. Sandwell, the editor of *Saturday Night*, wrote: "There will be no dearth of televiewers from the very beginning of the first...programme. The major task is to see that there are telethinkers at both ends of the wondrous process. Thinkers at just one end — no matter which end it is — will be ultimately disastrous." B.K. Sandwell was a wise man.

Other Books of Interest from James Lorimer & Company

Canada and the Reagan Challenge
Crisis and Adjustment, 1981-1985
Stephen Clarkson

Stephen Clarkson has revised his acclaimed 1982 study of Canada-U.S. relations to take in the final years of the Trudeau administration and the new Mulroney government. *Canada and the Reagan Challenge* is winner of the Canadian Anthropology and Sociology Association's 1984 John Porter Book Award.

"A document of extraordinary importance." — *Canadian Forum.*

"Canadians, including the Prime Minister, should read, or reread this book" — Patrick Martin, *Globe and Mail.*

Canada's Cultural Industries
Broadcasting, Publishing, Records and Film
Paul Audley

For both English and French Canada, Paul Audley provides a wealth of information on the state of the cultural industries: newspapers, magazines, books, recording, radio, television and film. Audley pays particular attention to problems of Canadian content and control, and how government could formulate new policies to strengthen these vital industries.

Canada's Video Revolution
Pay-TV, Home Video and Beyond
Peter Lyman

Satellite broadcasting, pay-TV, videodisc, videotext, personal computers, videocassette recorders and videogames present a challenge to the Canadian broadcasting, recording, film and publishing industries. Communications consultant Peter Lyman describes the impact of the new technology on Canadian culture, and details the strategies that must be adopted to make our cultural industries competitive and Canadian.

Just Watch Me
Remembering Pierre Trudeau
Larry Zolf

In six provocative essays, sharp-eyed, sharp-witted broadcaster Larry Zolf reviews fifteen years of Trudeau in power. Zolf's irreverent and insightful musings are complemented by his own selection of more than 70 pages of pictures of the photogenic PM, captioned by Zolf to capture the essence of "Mr. Reason Above Passion."

Two Nations
Susan Crean and Marcel Rioux

This book, subtitled "An essay on the culture and politics of Canada and Quebec in a world of American pre-eminence," is the fruit of an all-too-unusual collaboration. Marcel Rioux is a distinguished Quebec historian, perhaps best known for the seminal *Quebec in Question*. Susan Crean is a writer and broadcaster active in English Canada's cultural politics. Together, they address questions about the survival of English-Canada and Quebec that are usually discussed in isolation by each of the "two nations."

"Two hard-nosed dreamers who deserve to be heard." — Ottawa *Citizen*.

Bassett
Maggie Siggins

This telling biography of John Bassett provides a fascinating behind-the-scenes look at the worlds of politics, publishing, business and sports. Maggie Siggins interviewed more than 200 of Bassett's friends, family, business associates, critics and enemies to piece together a public career that includes masterminding the rise and fall of the Toronto *Telegram* and the building of a media empire.

"Bassett's information on the sport-newspaper-and-TV business world is first-rate, indeed excellent." — Larry Zolf, *Montreal Gazette.*

"This is an important book because it documents the cynicism and opportunism which too often prevail among our publishing and broadcasting moguls." — *Globe and Mail.*

Voyage of the Iceberg
The Story of the Iceberg that Sank the Titanic
Richard Brown

This book has established Richard Brown in the ranks of Canada's distinguished nature writers. It is the story of the *Titanic,* and of history's most infamous iceberg. But there is much more in *Voyage of the Iceberg.* As the iceberg makes its way from Baffin Bay to the fateful meeting in the North Atlantic, it passes through many other lives — of Inuit, whales, whalers and sealers — that Brown portrays in quiet, compelling prose. The acclaim this richly illustrated book has received in Canada has been echoed by its success in American and British editions.

"Lilting, lyrical and loving...a smashing little book." — Vancouver *Province.*

Willie: A Romance
Heather Robertson

Heather Robertson's historical novel about Mackenzie King and Ottawa during the national trauma of the Great War has been welcomed with accolades from all corners. It has been described as "brilliant" (*Maclean's*), "totally charming, funny and real" (*Chatelaine*), a triumph" (William French, *Globe and Mail*) and "a Canadian *Gone With the Wind*" (Montreal *Gazette*).

"The most extraordinary Canadian book of this fall season...rich, detailed and vivid." — Peter Gzowski, CBC *Morningside*.

"A fascinating, entertaining, and important book that carries the unmistakable stamp of a true writer's passion." — *Books in Canada*.